BUILDING

LEAN

COMPA

T0165809

HOW TO KEEP
COMPANIES PROFITABLE
AS THEY GROW

HANS D. BAUMANN

Morgan James Publishing • New York

BUILDING LEAN COMPANIES

by Hans D. Baumann © 2009 all rights reserved.

Library of Congress Control Number: 2008936938
ISBN: 978-1-60037-488-3   (Paperback)

Published by:
Morgan James Publishing, LLC
1225 Franklin Avenue Suite 325
Garden City, NY 11530-1693

Toll Free 800-485-4943
www.MorganJamesPublishing.com

Cover & Interior Design by:
3 Dog Design
www.3dogdesign.net

General Editor:
Heather Campbell

Contents

Dedication

To my wife, Sigrid, for her help and inspiration, and to Professor Fred Kaen for providing data and for his valuable critique.

Introduction

During my many years of working in managerial positions in small as well as in large multinational corporations, I observed that whenever a company grew, it increased sales and profits. However, this never happened at the same rate. I noticed that the percentage of profit on sales kept declining, indicating a reduction in operating efficiency.

I always wondered, what was the cause? Are there eventual limits to the growth of companies? After all, when the percentage of profit reaches zero, companies go bankrupt.

All living things die eventually; they don't grow or exist forever. Why then shouldn't companies die as well when they stagnate with age, or grow too big? Accepting such a premise is not as absurd as it sounds.

While companies don't have to abide by the biological, physical, or chemical laws that dictate life spans in living things, there are nevertheless, perhaps, not-yet-discovered laws or relationships that eventually cause a company's profitability to decline. Whatever such laws are, they invariably are based on human behavior. In other words, the profit—and therefore the fate—of companies quite often depend on the actions of the people who manage them and who work there.

That companies fail does not surprise us. After all, the world is full of firms that declared bankruptcy or otherwise went out of business. Think of Studebaker, RCA, Woolworth, and Pan Am, to name a few. Just consult any old business directory from the 1900s, and you will find only a handful of companies that are still around. Yet, age in itself is no cause for business failure.

So, then, what *are* the factors causing companies to fail? This book attempts to answer this question. As to loss of efficiency, there are in fact *three* questions to be answered. First, is there a difference in profitability between small and large companies? Second, does the efficiency (expressed as percentage of profit on sales) of companies decrease when they grow larger? Finally, what action can company management take to avoid such a fate?

Besides the obvious reasons why companies fail, such as incompetent management, lack of resources, or product obsolescence, there are some less understood reasons. Number one on my own list is excessive size of a company (referring to vertically integrated[1] companies only). Excessive growth can create effects similar to those caused by cancer in living organisms; in this case, the "cancer" is corporate bureaucracy. Vertical growth can bring with it too many reporting layers between president and workers, which severely limits the speed and accuracy of communication flow, among other detriments. Mistakes result in finger-pointing along the line, and real culprits often remain anonymous. Things get dicey at the front office when those who should be reporting to a company president—VPs of sales, manufacturing, engineering, marketing, and personnel—are replaced by those with special interests in shareholder relations, environmental concerns, affirmative action, and legal matters.

As early as 1933, Frank Knight[2] observed that there seem to be admonishing returns (reduced margins) when companies grow too big. He further elaborated that the relationship between efficiency and company size is one of the most serious problems. This question is particularly vital because the profit offered is a very powerful incentive to keep a firm expanding. Yet this profit incentive gets offset by an equally powerful effect: the resultant decrease in (managerial) efficiency, or increase in transaction cost.

Similar arguments apply when a firm has to choose between manufacturing all products in-house and purchasing all or a portion of parts from a subcontractor. The so-called economy of scale may be sacrificed if parts are produced externally. However, such assumed loss in profit may

---

1 Where a company has a single reporting structure starting at the top floor and ending at the president's office.
2 Oliver E. Williamson and Scott Masten, *The Economics of Transaction Costs: An Elgar Critical Writing Reader* (Northampton, MA), 181.

well be offset by the savings in internal governance cost and, of course, savings in capital otherwise spent on tools and equipment. Such reasoning has always proved correct in my own business experience.

As in the wild, where predators devour old and weak animals, so will younger and more agile competitors force large and inefficient companies out of business unless such companies have monopolistic market positions. Bigness, on the other hand, does have many advantages, economy of scale being one of them. But as we shall see, there are limits to such beneficial effects, and in the end, unstoppable growth of overhead will overpower everything else. Aside from its financial impact, it will slow decision making and product development, and finally hamper risk taking.

Nevertheless, one can learn to avoid, or at least reduce, the detrimental by-products associated with company growth. After all, growth is a natural and generally desirable goal. Company growth is a sign of virility and is good for the morale of employees and shareholders alike. What we should strive for, though, is to grow wisely. One should avoid too many reporting layers and keep one's organization flexible (organization charts, for example, should be frowned upon). Finally, a company should split up and grow horizontally once it has reached a certain size.

One should keep in mind that there is an important distinction between organic growth (such as that due to an increase in market share) and growth in sales due to inflation. The latter is not true growth, as I define it here, because there is basically no need to increase personnel during times of purely inflationary sales increases.

Why is there scant attention paid to the efficiency of a company's administrative organization, in contrast to the great resources spent to increase the productivity of direct labor? Just think of such buzzwords as "lean manufacturing." Well, I believe that there are three reasons: first, because CEOs derive most of their income from stock bonuses, their main concern is with "shareholder value"—in plain English, the price of their companies' stock. Shareholders do pay attention to "direct" labor cost (part of "cost of revenue"). Secondly, most CEOs are not technically qualified to understand the organizational intricacies of a complex corporate structure, a situation made worse by the fact that the average head of a company lasts only five years in a job, which is much too short a time to learn what needs to be known. Thirdly, there is no known way—in contrast to the case with factory workers—to measure the efficiency of an office employee or manager.

In this book, I propose certain scaling factors in order to model the growth in reporting layers and the number of managerial positions as a function of firm size. Such scaling-factor effects on businesses were also suggested by, among others, Jerry Useem in an article entitled "—GET BIGGER," which appeared in the April 30, 2007 issue of Fortune magazine.

However, the concept of applying scaling factors in order to estimate, for example, the relationship between productive to overall employees of a given firm, should not be taken literally. It is a rough guide only, and it certainly does not apply to all types of businesses. After all, no two businesses are organized exactly alike.

Take Wal-Mart, for example, which is a huge company with nearly two million employees. Why is it still in business? Because it considers every store a separate profit center (almost a separate company). Other examples where scaling rules may not apply are franchise businesses such as chains of fast-food restaurants. Here, the parent company simply collects franchise fees and sells supplies, while each restaurant is an independent operating entity. In companies that are heavily capitalized yet require little manpower, such as those in the chemical industry, any reduction in the level of bureaucracy has little impact on the bottom line, as will be explained later. Nevertheless, the concept of using scaling factors can give us a clue as to why certain (vertically organized) companies become overburdened by less productive office employees (in other words, by overhead).

This could be a valuable guide for any CEO who wants to at least maintain his percentage of profit on sales while his business expands.

The book makes a strong case for decentralized, divisionalized (horizontally organized) firms, which tend to avoid the seemingly unavoidable decrease in operating efficiency associated with the growth of rigid, centralized organizational structures.

Finally, as the reader will see, I use the percentage of profit on yearly sales as a yard-stick for company efficiency. This is in contrast to the measures employed by Wall Street, which uses price-earning ratios, free cash flow, gross profit margins, margins of earnings before interest, taxes, depreciation, and amortization," and others. In the final analysis, all these measures depend on the final figure stated on the bottom line of a profit-and-loss statement. If there is no profit, then everything else accounts for little. So why not start from there?

CHAPTER

1

Why Smaller Can Be Better

If it were true that smaller is better, then a flea would be a better animal than an elephant. — **Peter F. Drucker**

From an emotional point of view, I certainly agree with the above statement. After all, elephants don't bite, and they certainly look much better than fleas. Nevertheless, the flea can outperform the elephant ounce for ounce when it comes to physical power. Why is this, and does the same relationship apply to businesses?

To say that smaller companies can be more profitable sounds like heresy in an age that glorifies mergers and big business. Certainly, a larger company has more sales and typically more profit than a smaller enterprise, but what we usually don't see is that the percentage of profit on sales of a very large enterprise is usually lower than that of a smaller or midsize competitor. In other words, small or medium-sized enterprises tend to be more efficient than their larger brethren. We may be better able to understand why this is by observing nature.

In nature, we see distinct differences in metabolism and work performed per given time between smaller and larger animals, all following so-called scaling laws, which define the rate of metabolism per unit of body weight between larger and smaller animals. These laws also govern the ratio between the surface area and the volume of a sphere. Could such scaling laws apply to businesses?

For modeling purposes, one could consider that, like the surface area of a sphere, the number of *effective* (i.e., profit-producing) employees—factory workers, for example—increases only to the square of the diameter, while the total number of employees (including production and office workers) increases proportionally to the cube of the diameter, much like the volume of the sphere, as I will explain later.

Hence, the larger the company gets, the smaller the number of effective employees compared to the overall number of workers. As a result, the rate of profit (the margin) decreases. Some companies are quite aware of this problem and try to correct it. Take General Electric, for example, whose net earnings increased from 11% to 12.6% of sales between 2004 and 2006. Yet, it could only do this by severely pruning its overhead expenses from 35.2% to 24.8 % of sales. Without this drastic measure, its 2006 earnings would have shrunk to only 2.2% of sales!

Scaling Factors in Nature

Scaling laws in nature regulate certain physical phenomena and behavior. Some of us have experienced dust storms driven by forty- or fifty-mile-per-hour winds. Luckily for us, the sand particles we feel are rather small, averaging less than five one-hundredths of an inch in diameter. Larger stones—those, say, one-half inch in diameter—stay on the ground. The reason is that the stones obey the 2/3 power scaling factor, or the "prin-

---

3 Thompson, D'Arcy, *On Growth and Form* (Cambridge, UK: Cambridge University Press, 1966).

ciple of similitude," as D'Arcy Thompson[3] called it in his 1917 book *On Growth and Form*.

"It often happens," Thompson writes, "that of the forces in action in a system some vary as one power and some as another, of the … magnitudes involved." Thus, returning to our sandstorm example, a half-inch-diameter stone weighs 1000 times more than the average grain of sand because the volume and weight vary to the third power.

However, the same stone exposes just 100 times greater surface area to the wind than the grain of sand because surface area varies only to the second power. Hence, the larger stone has only 10 percent of the surface area per ounce than the smaller one. The wind pressure must therefore increase by ten times to lift the larger stone!

Scaling factors affect the animal kingdom, too. A smaller animal has proportionally more surface area than a larger one, approximating the ¾ power-scaling factor (see explanation later). More surface area means that more thermal energy is radiated away from the surface of the animal, allowing for more work to be done in the form of muscle movement in a given time period. The transfer of heat through the radiation of thermal energy results from a temperature differential that provides the thermodynamic potential for work. The more efficiently heat is continuously radiated, the more power can be produced. A smaller body with a larger surface area does this more efficiently. This is also reflected by the differences in caloric requirements between different-sized animals. As stated by Thompson, a man weighing seventy kilograms consumes thirty-three calories per kilogram in a day, while a whale weighing 150,000 kilograms consumes about 1.7 calories per kilogram of its own weight per day.

People experience this power-scale relationship whenever we work in the tropics, where we find that our rate of work slows down considerably without the benefit of air conditioning. This means that it would take us perhaps twice as long to dig a ditch as it would up north (we perform the same work while using only half the power). The reason is that while we have an unchanged surface area, the temperature difference is lower between our body temperature and that of the surrounding air. Therefore, less thermal energy can be radiated and less muscle power produced. We would notice the same effect if our body surface were somehow reduced while our weight remained the same. This is exactly what happens to obese people even in moderate climates. Conversely, a very lean person has relatively more radiating body surface and therefore can produce more power per ounce of body weight, as photographs of the winners of the Boston Marathon illustrate.

To take another example, a mouse weighs about one ounce (0.0625 pounds) while a man may weigh 160 pounds. Assuming a ¾ power scaling factor, the surface area—and thereby the metabolic rate—of the mouse is about seven times greater than that of a human per ounce of body weight. D'Arcy Thompson and others have shown that the absolute work output (which is different than the power output) per ounce of body weight is roughly the same in all animals. It follows from the simplest definition of work (weight times distance) that, say, a flea, a man, or an elephant jumping seven inches straight up (a feat of which each is capable) will produce about the same work *per unit weight*.

This prompts the question: if the work done is the same, why then is the power output of smaller animals higher? Why is the metabolic rate higher in smaller mammals than in larger ones? The answer is that the former can perform the same amount of work *much faster*. Power is, after all, defined as work per unit time. Calories are converted into power, or work per second. In theory, 192,000 mice (which collectively would weigh the same as one elephant) would be able to move a given object a certain distance in one second, whereas it would take the elephant twenty-one seconds to do the same!

In another example, an elephant can carry a log weighing no more than about 1,100 pounds. Fifteen men can carry the same log (about seventy pounds for each) the same distance and in the same time as an elephant does. Yet it would take seventy men to equal the weight of an average elephant. This shows that a man is, pound for pound, about 445 percent more power efficient than an elephant.

Scaling Factors and Businesses

Just as Adam Smith's "invisible hand" regulates markets, could the equivalent of natural scaling factors affect the profitability of businesses? Can it be that bigger is not necessarily better? All companies want to grow—a quite healthy thing to do—but how should they go about growing in the most profitable way?

Just as scaling factors apply to mice and elephants, could it not be that a smaller, homogenous manufacturing enterprise could be more power efficient, producing more widgets in a given time period than a larger counterpart?

Scaling laws, when applied to businesses, suggest that profit does not increase in linear proportion to sales growth or business size, but rather at a lesser, exponential rate. This rate could be defined by a power-scaling factor.

Using the ¾ power scaling factor, we could postulate that a company with 100 employees could produce the same number of widgets per employee as a competitor with 1,000 employees, but $(100/1000)^{3/4}$ / $(100/1000) = 1.78$ times faster. Expressed differently, six plants of the smaller variety could produce the same number of widgets per month as a single plant ten times as big. The reason for this is that more people in the larger plant work in jobs unrelated to the actual production of widgets, and each of the actual production workers in the large plant can only produce as many widgets in a given time period as their counterparts in the smaller plants. Expressed differently again, the larger plants have more overhead (and therefore higher transaction costs) due to the larger number of administrative workers. If this calculation holds true, then smaller, homogeneous enterprises (single, independent profit centers with their own management and accounting systems, and without any subdivisions or subsidiaries) will be more profitable, because they tend to have less overhead.

For our purposes, scaling laws may be usefully employed to help predict certain maximum size relationships within fully integrated (homogeneous) firms, although they certainly will not prevent the incompetent management of a small firm from resulting in a dismal profit picture. On the other side of the coin, a large enterprise might have an exceptionally large profit due to its quasi monopoly in a given business. Such cases should be excluded from this analysis.

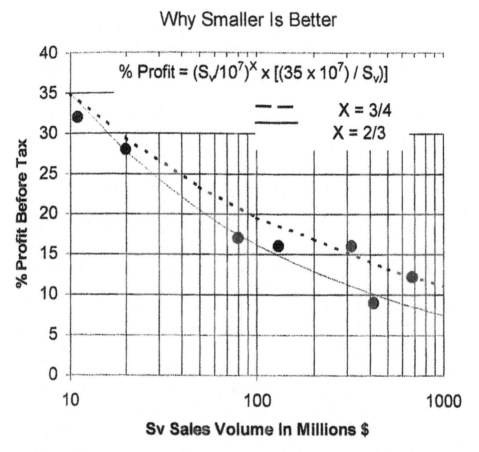

Why Smaller Is Better

$$\% \text{ Profit} = (S_v/10^7)^X \times [(35 \times 10^7) / S_v)]$$

X = 3/4
X = 2/3

Figure 1-1

Figure 1-1 shows a typical relationship. Here I plotted the pretax earnings, expressed in percentage of sales against annual sales volume, of manufacturing companies that are in the same (or a closely related) market and that are either homogeneous organizations or independent divisions of larger firms. The reference values shown for the calculations were arbitrarily chosen to match the $10-million sales point at a 35 percent profit. A 2/3 and a ¾ power factor are used because both factors appear in nature.

The proposed equation that can be used to predict the percentage of profit as a function of sales at a larger firm using a known reference profit at a smaller (reference) firm with a given smaller sales volume is:

% profit = (projected sales/reference sales)^E × reference profit at reference sales × reference sales/projected sales

Here is an example: At a given company, we have $10,000,000 in sales and a 35 percent profit. What will the profit be at $100,000,000 in sales?

% profit (at 100 Million) = (100,000,000/ 10,000,000)$^{0.75}$ × 35 × 10,000,000/100,000,000
% profit = 5.62 × 3.5 = 19.65 %

(E = exponential scaling factor, here taken as 0.75.)

Note that this equation is not applicable if the growth in sales volume is primarily due to monetary inflation—that is, price increases. In those instances, there are no basic increases in personnel, and hence there is no profit deflator. This situation arises in large and mature companies where the profit level over the years stays basically constant, except for economically caused business disruptions.

In a January 12, 1999 *New York Times* article entitled "Of Mice and Elephants: A Matter of Scale," it was stated that Max Kleiber, in the 1930s, found that metabolic rate scales with body mass not with the originally assumed power, but closer to the ¾ power. I therefore superimposed a curve following the ¾-power scale onto figure 1-1. The data points fall somewhere close or unknown in between. Nevertheless, both scaling factors clearly show a trend away from greater efficiency when a homogenous enterprise—or, for that matter, a conglomerate with equally growing divisions—expands. Note that the economy-of-scale effects do not appear in the data shown in figure 1-1 due to the lack of mass-produced items in this particular chosen industry.

Why, then, do larger corporations exist, and why do they make a decent rate of profit? This is because they are typically not homogenous organizations (i.e., one factory under one roof), but conglomerations of several semi-independent organizations, each with its own profit and sales numbers. In its structure, such a company resembles a strand of pearls (see figure 1-2). If such horizontally organized companies grow mostly through mergers and acquisitions, then their average rates of profit on sales will remain about the same.

Figure 1-2 shows seventeen individual divisions of a conglomerate with a total yearly sales volume of $1.581 billion and a total average profit of 11.5 percent. If this corporation were to add one more division with a sales volume of $120 million and a profit rate of 14 percent, then the overall average profit rate would be 11.7 percent, reflecting hardly any change at all. Clearly, no scaling factors apply here unless each division grows by itself and then becomes subject to its own scaling factors.

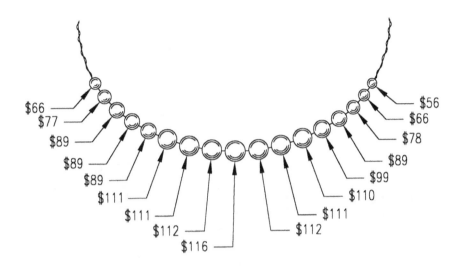

$66
$77
$89
$89
$89
$111
$111
$112
$116

$56
$66
$78
$89
$99
$110
$111
$112

Figure 1-2

Schematic depiction of a conglomerate with seventeen separate divisions

Even multidivisional companies can experience the slow erosion of their pretax profits due to the scaling effects in their growing divisions. An example of such a case is shown in figure 1-3. Here, the after-tax earnings of a well-run U.S.-based corporation is plotted showing rather impressive growth over the years.

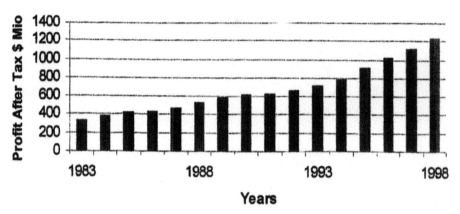

Figure: 1-3

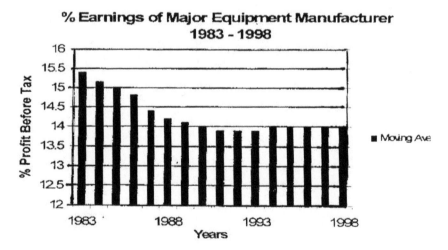

Figure: 1-4
Tax rates: 1993=43.9%, 1998=36.1%
Difference between pre-,and after tax rate showing hidden loss of efficiency.

However, if we examine the company's earnings before tax, as plotted in figure 1-4, we see a gradual erosion in profit as a percentage of sales, indicating a reduction in operating efficiency. The reason is that the effective tax rate of this company decreased from 44 to 36 percent over the given period, which masked the actual reduction in operating efficiency and the resultant pretax earnings decrease.

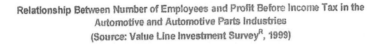

Relationship Between Number of Employees and Profit Before Income Tax in the Automotive and Automotive Parts Industries
(Source: Value Line Investment Survey[R], 1999)

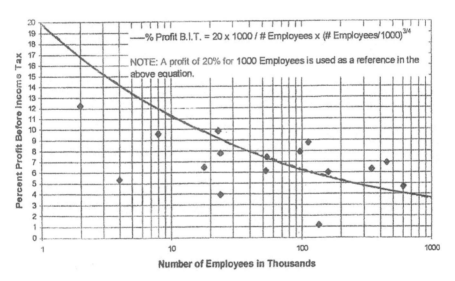

Number of Employees in Thousands

Figure 1-5

The gradual erosion of profit also occurs when overall employment increases. In figure 1-5, I plotted total employment against pretax profit for automobile companies (see also chapter 8) and their suppliers to illustrate this point. All of these companies, the largest of which included General Motors (the largest employer), Ford, and Volvo, are listed on U.S. stock exchanges. On the smaller employment scale are parts suppliers. This is a fair comparison, because all these companies are essentially in the same business and undergo similar competitive and labor-related pressures. The solid line is the predicted trend of all data points using the ¾ scaling law (assuming a 20 percent profit for 1,000 employees as an arbitrary starting point).

Although there is a lack of information on the low side, the available data shows an unmistakable trend toward lower profit as employment numbers increase, despite the fact that the larger corporations employ quite a number of financially independent divisions. However, in my opinion, they should have even more independent divisions in order to improve profit. As figure 5-1 shows, there is quite a scattering of data. One might deduce, for example, that the point at the intersection of 9 percent earnings and a hundred thousand employees likely represents either a foreign company or a company divided into several divisions. In contrast, the data point showing only 1 percent profit most likely represents a strongly centralized company.

The same relationship is applicable to cases other than those involving manpower and profit . An example is the efficiency of finding oil as a function of funds expended for drilling and other development expenses. As in other industries, we have recently seen major consolidations in the oil sector. The merger between Exxon and Mobil is one example. The purported reasons are to reduce staff expenses and to pool resources for oil exploration, all of which supposedly benefit shareholders.

Alas, the opposite may happen. According to Bill Fairhurst,[4] such mergers do not increase the value of the new company any more than the sum of the individual parts, nor have new oil and gas resources been discovered that would satisfy our ever-increasing demands.

What's worse, most of the integrated multinational oil companies are unable to replace their yearly oil and gas production, while smaller, independent oil companies, according to Fairhurst, have a 131 percent replacement rate! He further stated that the much smaller independents add more reserves within the United States than all the multinational cor-

---

4 Fairhurst, Bill, "Why US Energy Policy and Wall Street Should Focus on US Independence," *Oil and Gas Journal* (2001).

porations combined. This is despite the fact that the larger corporations spend much more money on exploration. The data in figure 1-6, taken from Fairhurst's article, make this very clear. Here, four large multinationals and five large integrated companies spent an average of $1.70 per thousand cubic feet of gas equivalent (Mcfe) and were able to replace only 50 percent of their production. In contrast, smaller and midsize independents averaged 100 percent replacement at an average cost of only $1.30 per Mcfe. Even though the data points are naturally scattered, as one would expect, the alert reader may spot the scaling factors at work. The solid line superimposed onto this graph shows the predicted results.

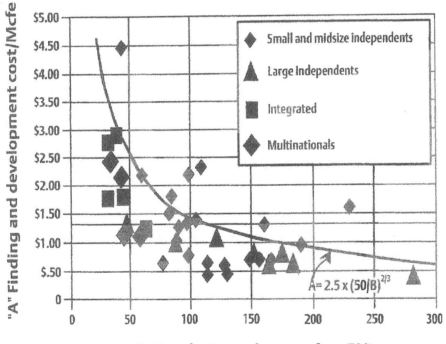

Figure 1-6

Finding/development cost for 37 companies when compared to results in % production replacement.

Why Is This Happening?

Is there a correlation between a company's sales volume and its profit, or one between its sales volume and its number of employees? Is there a connection between the number of employees and profit before tax? What is the real reason for such relationships??

One simple explanation is that as a company grows, its number of *effective*, or profit-producing, employees could vary as the second power of the relative size of the company while the number of *total* employees varies as the third power of the size. This mimics the relationship between the surface area and the volume of a sphere—hence the Law of the Sphere (see chapter 2). Mind you, the efficiency of an individual production worker in either a smaller or a larger plant is roughly the same. Inefficiency comes into play when the production worker in the larger plant has to support many more noneffective employees (administration, etc.) than the worker in the smaller factory. There is, of course, some compensation rendered for this by the economy of scale, in that some of the profit lost to overhead is regained through the increase in manufacturing productivity inherent in a larger factory (see chapter 3).

An organization chart can illustrate how efficiency and profitability can degenerate as companies grow. Let's start with the example of a single individual starting an enterprise with three production workers. His organization is shown in Figure 1-7A. Here, the ratio of production workers to overall employment is an impressive three to four, or 0.75. Let's call it 75 per-cent efficient.

After some growth, our man hires three foremen and six additional production workers (see figure 1-7B), thus maintaining the same 3:1 worker-to-boss relationship.[5]

---

5 I realize that a relationship of three workers per boss is not very realistic, but I chose it to simplify the chart.

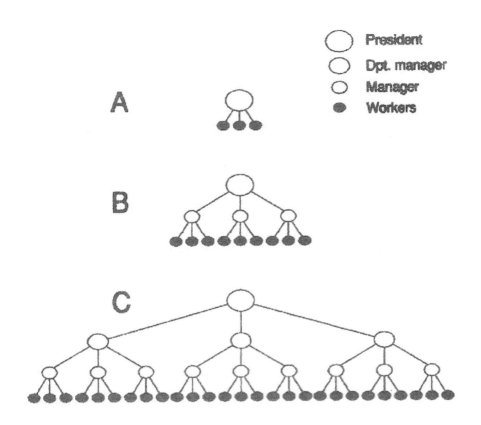

Figure 1-7

Simple organization chart of companies with one to three reporting levels.

However, the ratio between production and total employment has now decreased to 9:13, or 0.692—about 69 percent efficient.

As his company grows even further, his total employment swells to forty. Yet, even though the worker-to-boss ratio remains the same, his efficiency has decreased further, to 27:40, or 67 percent, as seen in Figure 1-7C.

Our example thus far has considered a very lean organization with no fat. But let's assume that our president in Figure 1-7B wants to add a secretary and a file clerk to his staff—quite a reasonable request. After all, his company has grown to a point at which he can no longer handle all the paperwork himself. The extra hires bring the overall employment from thirteen to fifteen persons, which decreases our ratio from 0.692 to 9:15, or 0.600, as shown in figure 1-8(B-1). We have just lost 9 percent efficiency!

Later on, he needs to expand his staff even further, commensurate with his increase in business. He adds six staff people in addition to hiring eighteen additional production workers. This certainly sounds fair, does it not? However, as figure 1-8(C-1) now shows, his ratio of production workers to overall employees is now down to 27:48, or 0.563—his plant efficiency has gone down to 56 percent!

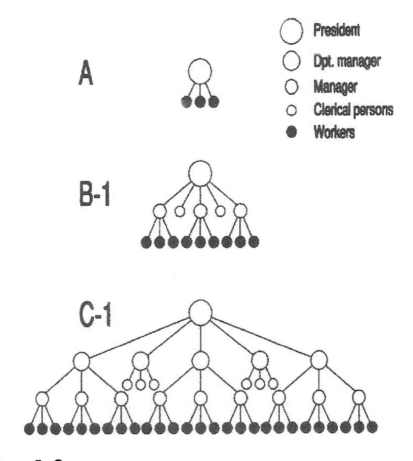

Figure 1-8

Organization chart of company with added clerical help.

What does all this mean to our budding entrepreneur? First, the good news. Growing from four employees (including himself) to forty-eight has increased his sales volume by $100 \times 27/3$, or 900 percent. Now, the bad news—his profit has grown by only $100 \times (56 \times 27)/(75 \times 3)$, which works out to 672 percent. Lowering his overall plant efficiency has cost him 25 percent of his potential profit!

This is the reality encountered by growing companies. It is nearly impossible to keep growing and maintain the same ratio between production workers and total employees that a desired constant operating efficiency (percentage of profit on sales) demands.

The above example also demonstrates how the Law of the Sphere operates: *Total employment grows at a higher exponential rate than the rate of growth of production workers ("effective" employees).*

But, like a cubic equation, the rate of decrease in the ratio diminishes as the number of reporting levels increases. The biggest decrease in the ratio—i.e., decrease in efficiency—occurs between the first and fourth reporting levels. Smaller changes occur thereafter. This, however, does not include the detrimental effects of adding clerical workers and additional staff layers to the organization (see figure 1-7). When these additions are taken into account, the efficiency ratio decreases much faster and at a less predictable rate.

A second reason, which is related to the above, may be that too many layers of management are created when organizations grow. These unnecessary layers can place a burden on support services analogous to the burden placed on the heart of an obese animal, which must pump significantly more blood to more tissues without any real increase in heart capacity. Having too many layers also severely restricts the communication flow from the decision-making top to the executing lower layers of the organization.

If we were to limit the number of management layers to four, which I consider optimal, and assume an average number of eight persons per department, the total number of employees of such a company could not exceed 4681! This is hardly a midsize plant.

A mathematical relationship implies that the further growth of such an enterprise under one roof would require additional layers of management. The detrimental effects of excessive management layers are widely known and have been discussed by the business writer Tom Peters, among others.

Third, does the effectiveness of communication decrease with size? The increasing number of departments may lead to an increasing number of decision makers on various levels within the hierarchy, which in turn produces invariable delays in, and watering down of, vital and—perhaps worse—even mundane business decisions (see chapter 4).

Fourth, there is invariably a proliferation of non-profit-contributing departments, which, while seemingly necessary—environmental and loss prevention departments are two examples—nevertheless leech vital company resources and manpower. These additional departments need managers, leading to a persistent increase in the number of managers in our economy, as the data in figure 1-9 clearly illustrate. It is instructive to see that the level of management stayed pretty constant in the 1960s and early 1970s, but started to rise rapidly in the early 1980s, after everybody in most offices started to have his or her own personal computer.

INCREASE IN MANAGEMENT OVER THE YEARS

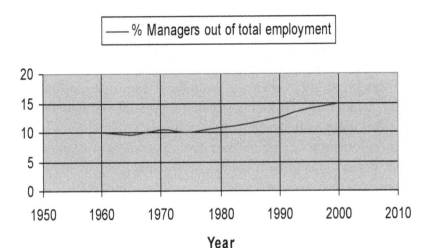

Source: US Bureau of Economic Analyses

Figure 1-9

What the above numbers imply is that practically one out of seven employees is a manager. This is about the same the ratio as that of officers to sailors in the U.S. Navy.

Fifth, business enterprise computer software gets exceedingly complex with larger organizations, and the cost of ownership soars.

Smaller businesses have organizational structures that offer a certain transparency that gets lost in larger companies. For example, the owner of a small auto repair shop with twenty-five employees knows quite well how his company is organized and what everybody is supposed to do. On the other hand, department managers in firms with several thousand employees—let alone the CEOs of such firms—are at a loss to understand or explain their enterprise system.

Finally, with growth we see a disappearance of the original entrepreneurial spirit and with it the *esprit du corps* or enthusiasm of a company's employees. It is easy to see that even major department managers in large firms spend more time maintaining the status quo or worrying about their own security than about their customers or their company's profitability. This can partially be countered with a proper profit-sharing plan or other incentives, although distributing such incentives fairly and equitably is more difficult in larger firms than in smaller ones.

At this point, the reader may wonder if I am ignoring the obvious benefits of large organizations, which are typically conglomerates. The truth is that these benefits are partly myths.

A conglomerate's combined purchasing power is often cited as a benefit, but it can actually be a detriment because it forces the company's divisions into the hands of a few monopolistic suppliers, resulting in an absence of competitive bidding and a vulnerability to strikes. As another example, a corporatewide research and development (R&D) department cannot possibly understand the technical complexity of each division's products. In the same vein, even legal support services should be subject to competitive bidding by local law offices.

Consider the following example of a conglomerate's ostensibly cost-saving idea. The firm's corporate headquarters, located in a major city, made a deal with a local travel agent to supply airline tickets to all of its divisions nationwide. In return, the agent would refund 5 per-cent of all fares to the corporation. The trouble was that the city where the head-quarters was located was the hub of one large airline, which, due to its near-monopoly, charged excessive fares. Needless to say, the local agent favored this carrier due to higher commissions, and so did the corporate headquarters, because it received 5 percent of all fares. The victims in all of this—besides the shareholders—were the CEOs of the divisions, because they were saddled with a 15 to 20 percent higher travel budget.

Lessons to be Learned

What can we learn from all of this? If we accept that smaller is better, then we can devise a strategy around this concept. First a rapidly growing company should make every effort to split its product lines into smaller, financially independent parts. The key to success, as always, is to find competent and well trained general managers. Do not put managers in charge who have been trained in a very large facility. Instead, try to hire a person who comes from a small firm run by an entrepreneur.

If you expand by acquisition, then leave the newly acquired organization alone unless its management was exceptionally poor. The corporate CEO of the parent company should make it his or her highest priority to avoid unnecessary interference by corporate staff people in the operation of divisions.

Scaling down the size of the parent headquarters will always be a good remedy for such problems. The same philosophy applies to mergers. Try to keep the production, marketing, and even the logo of each merger partner as intact as possible. The ultimate aim of all your actions as CEO should be to maintain, if not grow, the rate of profit—that is, the percentage of profit on sales—while your business is increasing.

As Dennis Meadows and his coauthors state in their book *Beyond the Limits*, our industrial production is still highly inefficient. Let's start to solve this problem by devising more efficient company management structures. This is where the real profit can be reaped.

We can already see this trend toward smaller and more efficient manufacturing plants. Mini steel mills replacing their nonprofitable larger predecessors comes to mind. As the editors of the Economist stated in their February 13, 1999 issue, "The future lies with smaller and more flexible factories, like the ones General Motors is building in Brazil and Michigan."

Other factories will follow the examples of the steel mills and auto plants as they are forced by competitive pressure to reduce overhead and stay profitable, or become so once again. Unfortunately, we now see this tend counteracted by a virtual "merger mania," in which efforts to make a killing on the stock market overcome all economic considerations.

One final thought: it is better for a single division to fail—be it due to mismanagement, litigation, or product obsolescence—than for its problems to be allowed to infect its parent firm. The potential negative financial impact for the large firm that ignores this rule is greater by far than even the complete loss of a small division.

CHAPTER

2

Law of The Sphere

Increases in manufacturing efficiency seldom keep up with increases in administrative expenses.

An old saying goes, "If you are not a liberal under thirty, you have no heart; if you are not a conservative over forty, you have no brain." I'd like to propose something similar: "If you don't believe in a centralized corporate structure when you are under thirty, you'll flunk your MBA exams; if you don't believe in a *de*centralized organization by the time you are forty, then you shouldn't start a business!"

There are, of course, exceptions. For example, a shipyard needing thousands of people under one roof to build a nuclear aircraft carrier can hardly be split into separate profit centers. But these should stay exceptions, and they should not distract from our aim to succeed with more and smaller individual profit centers instead of larger and more cumbersome single corporate enterprises.

Although I never attended a business school, I nevertheless was enthralled by the seemingly obvious economics of large combined corporate structures when I was a young man. After all, a large corporation has vast resources and a well-staffed R&D department that a small company could never afford, not to mention the clout of a corporate marketing and sales staff. In addition, it has the centralized purchasing power to put all kinds of cost-cutting pressure on its vendors. Finally, it has fewer competitors, thus allowing it a better pricing structure.

When I got older and had practical exposure to the ways smaller and larger companies worked, I found that, as is the case with large central governments, any technical efficiencies achieved by greater size were eaten away by problems with a company's "human factor." By this, I mean that individual employees tended to become depersonalized, the inefficiencies of multi layered management became stifling, and, worst of all, the constant attempts by middle management to accumulate staff and to build empires grew detrimental to the company's overall health.

When debating the issue of small versus large companies, one must distinguish between two categories of employees.

1. The *effective* employee
2. The *supportive* employee

Note that I use the term *effective* instead of *efficient.* A manager working in the environmental service department of a large corporation might be very efficient in writing letters to the federal government outlining plans to avoid spills, but this effort is not effective in increasing sales and profit. (This does not imply that the job is unnecessary—after all, a fine by the government can be costly and bad public relations.)

For the purpose of this study, I will categorize those employees whose work is not directly related to sales and production as *supportive.* This category includes employees in departments such as research and development, marketing, public relations, human resources, stock-holder relations, and others of this sort.

In his book *The Dilbert Principle*[1], Scott Adams defines non fundamental work done by supportive staff as:

- Quality fair
- Employee satisfaction survey
- Process improvement team
- Recognition committee
- Reorganization
- Writing mission statements
- Writing an approved equipment list
- Policy improvement
- Standards
- Suggestion system
- ISO 9000
- Writing vision statements
- Budget process

He further defined non fundamental work as "any activity that is one level removed from your people or your product."

In looking at the above list, most sensible people would readily agree that the majority of the stated activities are not necessary and usually the result of popular fads. However, the larger the company, the more unnecessary activities are tolerated or deemed "politically correct."

It is difficult to measure the output of employees who work in supportive departments, but their success is usually related to the effectiveness of their supervisor. Such effectiveness is impaired if there is not enough backup work. An employee not knowing what to do when a work assignment is completed will produce "rubber work." In the words of C.N. Parkinson[2], "Work expands to fill the time available." Effectiveness is also impaired if the supervisor does not have the technical background to understand the work he assigns. He is then at the mercy of his staff and is forced to believe in all real or imaginary problems that a project encounters.

Strictly considering their direct impact on the business performance of a company, effective employees are personnel involved in direct sales support, production (including direct production supervision), planning

---

1 Scott Adams, *The Dilbert Principle*, (Harper Collins, 1996)
2 C. Nortkote Parkinson, "Parkinson's Law," (Boston: Houghton Mifflin Co.), 1975.

and purchasing (strictly related to business inventories), and engineering as related to order-related efforts. In other words, an effective employee is any per-son whose effort leads directly to obtaining and executing a customer order and whose effort, therefore, has a direct impact on the profitability of the enterprise.

As you can see, my examples are related to manufacturing companies, in which the distinction between effective and supportive employees can most readily be made. However, a similar analysis should apply to other businesses as well.

A good manager is interested in having a high ratio of effective to supportive employees in his company—a high E/S ratio. Achieving this is his ticket to profitability. I strongly believe that control of the E/S ratio is the most important task of any chief executive officer. Growth in the *effective* category is usually business-related. If one's order volume increases, one first works overtime and later hires more personnel. This is a relatively easy task, and the whole process is nearly transparent. On the other hand, one must reverse the process when orders decrease, such as in a recession. First, one reduces working hours, and then one terminates positions. Unfortunately, the latter typically does not happen in the *supportive* category. Terminating supportive positions is usually an act of desperation when times are tough and the balance sheet is awash with red ink. Why is this true? Well, one reason is that administrative positions tend to become invisible compared to those involving hourly wages and widgets produced per hour. There are countless business studies on how to improve efficiencies in production, but hardly any on how to improve efficiencies of staff people[3]. How does one measure the efficiency of a marketing person? If it took ten people to come up with a brand name for a "new and improved" detergent, could five persons do just as well? Probably.

In my past association with medium-sized manufacturing companies, I was absolutely astonished to see management hire consultants to time-study the performance of the machine shop to determine the machining time of individual parts expressed in minutes to the fourth decimal place!

This was done even though the unionized workers made a point of slowing down the machine tool speed upon spotting the timekeeper.

We have a tremendous fascination with reducing direct labor (an expense that typically accounts for 18 percent of a product's selling price) by 5 or 10 percent, but we think nothing of increasing general and administrative (G&A) expenses by 2 percent (by hiring time keepers, increase planning staff, etc.) in order to reduce direct labor costs. Incidentally, a 10 percent decrease in direct labor increases profit by about 1.8 percent, while a 10 percent increase in G&A typically *decreases* profit by 2.7 percent.

The latest trend in reducing cost is to relocate machining facilities from the United States to other regions such as Mexico, Eastern Europe, and Asia. The reason is that most managers are fascinated by the direct wage differential—$15 per hour in Nebraska versus $3 per hour in Mexico, for example. This is a very superficial comparison. Because practically all modern tool machines are numerically computer controlled, their cost is rather high (several hundred thousand dollars each). The cost of the machine alone is typically $80 per hour due to depreciation of the purchase price alone. The real comparison between Mexico and the U.S. is, therefore, $80 + $3 versus $80 + $15. This will yield a real cost saving of 14.4 percent instead of the 80 percent one might expect—which is still not too bad.[4] However, to this we must add the costs of building a new plant, training new employees (among whom there is typically a high turnover in Mexico or China), relocating U.S. supervisors (at higher salaries), long-distance transportation, custom duties, extra inventories, and even such mundane items as finding trained mechanics to service the electronics. Relocating assembly operations, which require little more than low-cost manual labor with fewer expensive machine tools, makes much more sense. Nevertheless, all of a company's relocation studies

---

3 I remember one efficiency consultant recommending that staff people should be put in cubicles, which surely would improve efficiency in the office. Following the change, however, the same number of people still did the same amount of work. Where was the increase in efficiency? Strange, isn't it?

4 Note that the savings in profit are only 0.18 × 0.144, or 2.64 percent, since labor only constitutes about 18 percent of the selling price. This makes the choice even worse.

consume an awful lot of staff work and travel expenses—supportive costs that are typically not accounted for in the cost-cutting planning stage!

Let's return now to the problem of maintaining a decent ratio of effective to supportive personnel. One of the biggest problems a CEO faces is determining the optimum—or, better yet, the *absolute minimum*—number of staff or supportive personnel needed in his organization. This is a daunting task that gets more difficult the larger a company is, as its organizational structure becomes less and less transparent as it grows. Relying on one's department heads in this matter is usually futile. Typically, they will say things like, "We're already cut to the bone," or "We even had more employees during the '82 depression," or "Our marketing department is smaller than our competitor's. If we reduce our staff further, we won't be able to introduce new products."

The trend toward more electronic communication also tends to increase staff requirements. After all, somebody has to read all the extra reports that computer users generate. All this is a clear argument for decentralization and smaller-sized companies. Remind yourself that small is beautiful and small is profitable. If nothing else, it restores the transparency of a company's organizational structure to the eyes of the CEO.

Consider the chart in figure 2-1. It contains plotted performance data for metal fabricating and machining industries taken from *Value Line*[5] for the year 1994. I excluded companies with sales over $1 billion, because these companies are typically conglomerates of many smaller, quasi-independent companies and therefore would not be representative for this study. On the other hand, companies below $100 million in annual sales volume were not listed and therefore are not included.

The graph demonstrates two things: first, it reveals, amazingly, how many companies are satisfied with a profit before income tax (B.I.T.) of only 5 to 10 percent. Apparently, they consider it a success merely to be comparable to their competitors. Second, the chart shows a definite trend toward higher profit with decreasing sales—i.e., smaller company size.

---

5 *Value Line*, Value Line Publishing Inc., 1994.

For example, the average profit for companies with between $500 million and $1 billion in sales is 6.17 percent, but for those between $250 million and $500 million in sales, it's 8.4 percent, and for those between $100 million and $250 million in sales, it's 11.6 percent!

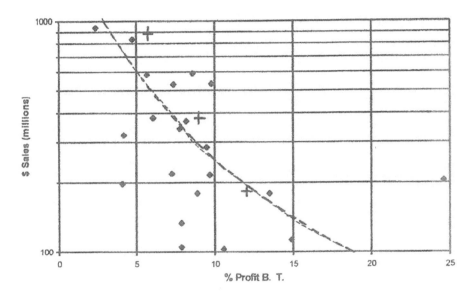

Figure 2-1

Relationship between sales and earnings before tax of small-to-medium sized companies (Source: ValueLine®, 1994 data) + = Average Values --- = Calculated values where % profit = $4(1000/Sales)^{23}$

One of the problems encountered by larger companies is the number of layers of management. In his excellent book *Thriving in Chaos*,[6] Tom Peters suggests limiting the number of management layers to no more than five, with between twenty-five and seventy-five people reporting to a manager. Except for purely clerical jobs (such as data entry in an insurance company), I personally consider more than twenty-five persons to be unmanageable for only one supervisor.

---

6 Thomas Peters, *Thriving in Chaos* (New York: A. Knopf, 1987).

Let's consider the components of an industrial company aside from its manufacturing department, which is usually not the problem in any organization. There are typically ten departments—sales, marketing, order entry, engineering, research and development, human re-sources, purchasing, planning, accounting, and customer service. Assuming that each is staffed with twenty-five persons, there would be 250 workers plus ten managers, equaling 260 employees, not including the CEO. This would be a three-layer company. If the company is larger, we find twenty-five subsections in each of the ten major departments of twenty-five people each.

However, the reality is that there are typically only four to twelve persons reporting to one supervisor or manager. Using an average size of eight per department, and with a maximum number of five management levels, we have to limit the size of the nonmanufacturing portion of any company to only $8^4 + 8^3 + 8^2 + 8$ and 1 CEO, for a total of 4681 employees! There are then only two ways to increase the company's size: (1) Increase the number of layers of management, or (2) split the company into several smaller, autonomous, divisions, each of which should operate in all but name as a completely separate company unfettered by the staff of the parent company.

Emerson Electric Corporation is one company that has successfully kept its divisions independent. Its financial results reflect the success of this effort. As its 2006 earnings statement proves, with $21.95 billion in sales, it achieved a respectable 12.2 percent profit before taxes, which, referring to figure 2-1, would place it somewhere in the earning range of a single company with about $200 million in sales volume. However, one should not overlook the fact that in 1996, this company had a 14.4 percent profit with only $11.1 billion in sales. *Sic transit gloria mundi!* Amazingly, though, Emerson closely followed the prediction of our Law of the Sphere, which would have predicted a 12.15 percent profit in 2006 (compared to the actual 12.2 percent result). Here, profit B.I.T. in 2006 = $(21.95/11.1)^{0.75} \times 14.4 \times (11.1/21.95) = 12.15$ percent.

The implied relationship between company size and profit extends also to separate divisions or different manufacturing facilities of larger enterprises. As stated in previous examples, there is plenty of evidence that smaller divisions typically outperform larger divisions within the same firm when it comes to percentage of profit on sales.

To call for smaller, leaner organizations is, of course, nothing new. In his book *Organization and Management in Industry and Business*,[7] originally published in 1928, William B. Cornell (incidentally, a fellow mechanical engineer) argued for centralized executive control even in small firms, which inadvertently limits the size of the organization, thus rendering it more controllable. If nothing else, this reduces the effect of "Management By Committee Syndrome."

There are exceptions, of course. For example, the Catholic Church hierarchy manages 407,750 priests worldwide[8] with only five management layers. Then again, it has had nearly 2000 years of practice and is a not-for-profit organization. Nevertheless, as Hammer and Champy[9] explain, when you need eleven people to produce 100 widgets a day, you need 193 people (instead of 110) in order to produce 1,000 widgets, due to the added support staff. Consider the United States Navy. A typical aircraft carrier needs 5,000 personnel to bring eighty aircraft into action, or more than sixty support people per plane. Using the same logic, a smaller aircraft carrier holding only forty planes would need only a crew of 2027, or only fifty-one persons per plane. Therefore, building two identical smaller carriers—which would still have a total of eighty planes—would save the navy 946 sailors.

An example of how a reduction in layers of management increases efficiency is given by Tichy and Sherman,[10] who reported that General Electric's lighting division reduced its layers of management from seven to four, with a resultant increase in sales per salaried employee of 35 percent!

---

7 William B. Cornell, *Organization and Management in Industry and Business* (New York: The Ronald Press Company, 1928).
8 *Welt Am Sonntag*, Hamburg, Germany, Feb. 23, 1997.
9 Hammer & Champy, *Reengineering the Corporation* (Harper Business, New York, 1996).
10 Tichy & Sherman, *Control Your Destiny or Someone Else Will* (Harper Collins, 1995).

Considering all this, wouldn't it be nice to have a mathematical tool to predict the relationship between size and profitability? A method that could predict the decrease in profit when the size of an organization is increased?

Microorganisms are an example from nature of smaller being better. Bacteria, for ex-ample, are incredibly small creatures consisting of only a single cell. Evolution, despite all the other changes that have taken place over the millennia, has kept them that small. The reason is that they basically constitute a sphere, the core of which contains only the basic elements for survival and procreation. They have no extra frills, yet they need a relatively large surface area to interact with other cells or substances. A small diameter gives them that advantage, an advantage that decreases the larger the sphere gets.

Consider the two spheres in figure 2-2. The smaller one has a radius of one inch, while the larger has a radius of two inches. The equations governing the surface area of a sphere, A, and the volume of a sphere, V, are given as follows:

$$A = 4 \times \pi \times r^2 = 12.56 \times r^2, \text{ and}$$
$$V = (4/3) \times \pi \times r^3 = 4.19 \times r^3$$

These equations show that a sphere's volume increases to the third power of the radius r. It does this at a much faster rate than the increase in the surface area of a sphere, which only increases to the square of the radius. The volume of the sphere with a two-inch radius is eight times larger than that of the one-inch-radius sphere. Yet the area increases only four times when the radius increases from one to two inches.

Another example is shown in figure 2-3. At a radius of ½ inch (1-inch diameter), the volume is about 0.52 cubic inches and the surface area is 3.14 square inches (giving a ratio of about 6:1). At a five-inch radius, the volume has increased to 524 cubic inches, while the surface area has only increased to 314 square inches (now the ratio is only 0.6:1). This proves that the volume, after the radius has increased by a factor of ten, has increased 1,000 times, while the surface area has only increased 100 times! No wonder bacteria want to stay small! They need a relatively large surface area to interact with adjacent cells while still utilizing a minimum-sized core, or support structure. The natural limit in the size of a bacterium is governed by the ability of the surface area to feed the core substance (the volume).

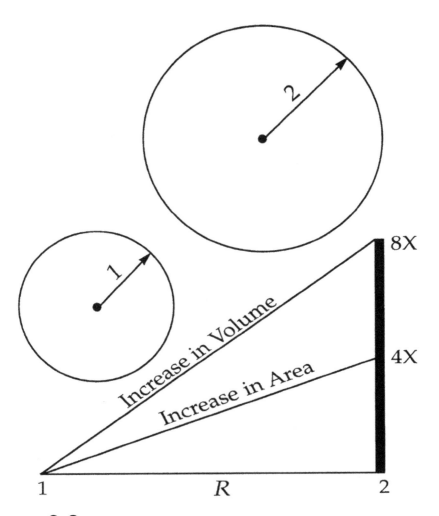

Figure 2-2

Relationship between size, volume, and surface area of differently sized spheres.

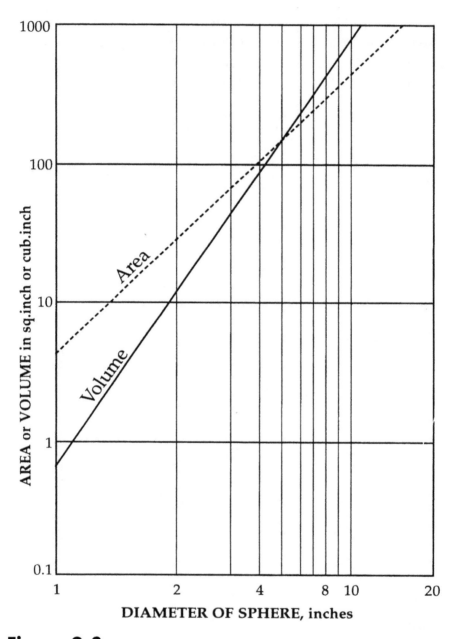

Figure 2-3

Example of how the rate of change between the volume and surface diverges.

The examples to the left show that the relationship between area increase and volume in-crease is expressed by $r^{2/3}$, or what I have been calling the Law of the Sphere.

What I suspect is that human organizations are also subject to this Law of the Sphere. We may compare the surface area of a sphere to that part of an organization that is actively involved in creating profit—the external sales force engaging the customer in a sales organization, or a soldier engaging the enemy if the organization is an army. In manufacturing, the surface area would include order fulfillment, direct-production labor, and so on—in other words, what I previously defined as an effective labor force.

The *volume* of the sphere, on the other hand, would comprise the total number of employees, including the previously identified supportive personnel. In private industry, this would include corporate headquarters, marketing, R&D, stockholder relations, and so on, in addition to manufacturing and sales. In an army, this would include staff and logistics, for example. Just like a bacterium, a good CEO wants a surface area as large as possible in relation to his unit's unavoidable volume. This, of course, predicates a small sphere—a small organization.

Does the Law of the Sphere, which tells us that the surface area only increases to the two-thirds power of the volume increase, really apply to human organizations? If so, it would follow that the effective number of employees, E_1, out of a given number of total employees, T_1, would increase to a new number of effective employees, E_2, by the two-thirds power of the ratio between the total new number of employees, T_2, to the old number, T_1. Expressed as an equation, $E_2 = E_1(T_2 / T_1)^{2/3}$.

In analyzing data accumulated from private sources and from business publications, I have found that at least a partial relationship exists, which, in many cases, while not as mathematically perfect as spheres, may be used to shed light on why organizations seem to lose their efficiency as they get larger.

For example, say a company has a total employment (T_1) of 100 people, out of which 60 people (E_1) would be in the effective category, and you wanted to double the size of the company to 200 people (T_2). The new number of effective personnel would only increase to $E_2 = 60$ $(200/100)^{2/3} = 95$ people instead of $2 \times 60 = 120$ people, as you might have guessed. As a matter of fact, in order to double the production—that is, to have 120 *effective* personnel (while ignoring any increases in productivity)—you have to increase the total employment of the firm to 285 people! However, a more realistic exponential factor for businesses would be ¾ (0.75), as previously discussed. This would increase the employment to 101 instead of only 95 people.

Let's get more specific and define the Law of the Sphere. From the previous area-to-volume relationship, $A_2/A_1 = (V_2/V_1)^{2/3}$, where the area of a second sphere is proportional to the area of a first sphere as given by the two-thirds power of the ratio between the volume of the second sphere to that of the first. This can now be generalized as follows:

The Law of the Sphere

The ratio between a number depending on a second variable to a number depending on a first variable is given by the two-thirds power of the ratio between the second and the first variable. Or, somewhat simplified: The ratio of one set of numbers is equal to the two-thirds power or the ratio of a second set of numbers:

$$A_2 / A_1 = (V_2 / V_1)^{2/3}$$

Now, if we want to know what A2 is, we can rearrange the equation as follows:

$$A_2 = A_1(V_2 / V_1)^{2/3}$$

Now let's apply this law to human organizations by substituting, for example, the number of total workers for volume and the number of effective workers for area. We can now determine the ratio between the two if a company grows—that is, if the total number of workers increases from size (1) to size (2). So, we may state:

$$\frac{\text{No. of effective workers (2)}}{\text{No. of effective workers (1)}} = \left[\frac{\text{No. of Total Workers (2)}}{\text{No. of Total Workers (1)}} \right]^{2/3}$$

Instead of dealing with individual persons, we may substitute a group of workers, such as a department. In this case, we could say that there are twelve total departments including seven effective departments in Plant A and twenty total departments in Plant B. Given this in-formation, what would be the number of effective departments in Plant B? The solution is:

$(20/12)^{2/3} \times 7 = 9.84$, or, when rounded off, ten effective departments.

We could even very easily apply this law to the military by substituting the number of effective units, such as army companies or divisions, for plant departments, as in the following example.

In 1997, there were approximately 495,000[11] men and women serving in the U.S. Army. Let's assume that the largest effective fighting unit (Y) is a division of about 14,000 soldiers. Looking at these numbers, you might assume that the total number of divisions (X) that can be fielded is 495,000 divided by 14,000—which, rounded off, is 35. Unfortunately, this number is not correct. Let's consult our Law of the Sphere. Here, $X = 1 \times (495,000/14,000)^{2/3} = 10.8$ divisions. This compares well with press reports of that period stating that the army had 10 combat-ready divisions. The above relationship sadly indicates that simply doubling the size of the army would not double the number of combat-ready divisions. It would only increase it to: $X = 1 \times (990,000/14,000)^{2/3} = 17.1$ or about 17 divisions, rather than 22. If we multiply the 10.8 divisions by 14,000 personnel each, we get 151,200 fighting personnel out of a total of 495,000, or one out of 3.3. Contrast this to the ancient Chinese army[12] circa 400

---

11 *The New York Times*, April 29, 1997.
12 Sun Tzu, *The Art of War*, (Oxford University Press, 1963), p 72.

BC, which had three fighting men out of every four. Incidentally, the low number of actual combat personnel in the U.S. Army explains the insufficient strength of our forces currently in Iraq. To compensate for this, the United States has had to enlist the help of the marines, the army reserves, and private contractors. The reserves, being composed of much smaller units linked to individual states, have fewer officers and therefore have more available combat personnel (see also chapter 4).

You may think, "Well, this is the government—private industry is much more efficient." Perhaps not. Consider, for example, the German Volkswagen Company. Ferdinand Porsche designed the original Volkswagen Beetle between 1934 and 1936, had the first prototype on the road in 1936, and oversaw the first production run of thirty cars, which were assembled by April 1937. He was able to do this with about fifty technicians and engineers at a cost (in today's dollars) of about $50 million.[13]

In contrast, in the 1970s, the Volkswagen Company employed about 50,000 engineers and technicians. Despite this, the company was unable to design a suitable replacement for the obsolete Beetle. In desperation, VW purchased a German competitor, Auto Union, and sold its so-called NSU design under the name of Rabbit. (Curiously, one could still see Auto Union's Olympic rings trademark on the Rabbit engines produced by VW during the first two years.) Why should this have been? Consider the Law of the Sphere. By increasing its engineering staff from fifty to 50,000, Volkswagen only increased its number of effective engineers by $(50,000/50)^{2/3} = 100$ times, instead of the thousand-fold increase it expected. Apparently, this was not enough.

Obviously, some companies might be more efficient than others and may be able to maintain a higher ratio of effective to supportive labor than indicated by the mathematical relationship of a pure sphere. However, I maintain that it is impossible for even the best manager to maintain a *constant* ratio as his company grows. What he may be able to do, rather, is maintain a larger exponential growth factor. Table 2-1 shows the

13 Hans Mommsen, "Das Volkswagenwerk und Seine Arbeiter im dritten Reich," *Econ Verlag*, 1966.

mathematical relationship assuming the worst, or basic, exponent factor of 2/3, as dictated by the Law of the Sphere as previously discussed (A), and a factor of ¾ (B). It shows how the number of effective employees (labor) increase as function of total employment growth.

Table 2-1

The relationship between increases in effective labor and overall employment.

A) Standard efficiency organization, $n = 2/3$ as per the Law of the Sphere

If total employment is increased by a factor of:	2	5	10	20	50	100
Then effective labor increases by a factor of:	1.6	2.9	4.6	7.4	13.6	21.5

B) Better efficiency organization, $n = ¾$

If total employment is increased by a factor of:	2	5	10	20	50	100
Then effective labor increases by a factor of:	1.7	3.3	5.6	9.5	18.8	31.6

From what I consider an optimum baseline—namely, sixty-five effective persons out of a total employment of 100—and using the data from Table 2-1(B), which is probably more realistic than (A), we can now derive the exact number of effective workers in a total workforce, as well as its E/S ratio (the ratio of effective to supportive workers).

Table 2-2

Total employees	100	200	500	1000	2000	5000
Effective employees	65	111	217	365	614	1222
Supportive employees	35	87	283	635	1386	3778
E/S ratio	1.86	1.25	077	0.57	0.44	0.32

As you can see, there has to be a dramatic increase in production efficiency for the effective workers in plants with over 500 people to make up for the drastic increase in overhead (the number of supportive employees.) *Hence, increases in manufacturing efficiency seldom keeps up with increases in administrative expenses.*

The above table also demonstrates quite vividly why smaller companies are able to compete successfully against industrial giants, at least in businesses that don't require huge capital investments.

The question for any CEO is: What category does his or her company fall under? One source for the answer is obviously the company's profit-and-loss statement. A low profit before interest and taxes usually means a bad ratio between effective and supportive personnel. As a rule of thumb, if you have a single plant or division with about $20 million in sales, and if your operating profit before tax is 2 percent or less, then you definitely have a low efficiency exponent. If profits are closer to 10 percent, you probably fall into the better category. With profits exceeding 15 percent, you are certainly in the optimum efficiency category. There may, of course, be extenuating circumstances that distort your profit picture—a strike or a recession, for example. Therefore, it is best to use five-year averages for your calculations. Of course, you can throw this book away if you run a multibillion-dollar-per-year software business as a monopoly. Business efficiency is of no concern if you can dictate your price.

Now back to us folks who have to compete. Another way to evaluate your firm is to divide the effective number into the total number of employees. Use 100 total and 65 effective as a basis,[14] then consult table 2-1 to see where you stand.

For example, if your total workforce is 980, of which 310 are classified as effective, then you can assume that your total employment has increased by 980/100 = 9.8 times, and the number of effective workers by 310/65 = 4.8 times, using the benchmark numbers of 100 and 65 from the first column of table 2-2. Looking at table 2-1, we find that in Group A, the effective increase for a tenfold increase in employment is 4.6. In Group B, it is 5.6. Therefore, you fall somewhere in between the two.

The base figures of 100 for total and 65 for effective employees are somewhat arbitrary and would certainly vary by industry. If you run a multidivisional enterprise, then you could use its smallest or most efficient division as a baseline in order to do a similar analysis.

The main point here is that, as with living organisms, there is an inherent law in business stating that growth and efficiency cannot be scaled up at the same rate.

To keep growing while outperforming the Group B numbers takes the talent of a superb manager. Simply increasing one's profit with increasing sales is not enough. Being able to increase profits *at the same rate as that of company growth* is what separates a truly great manager from a mediocre one.

Returning to business, here is an example of a valve and fitting business listed on the New York Stock Exchange and run by a very capable CEO. His growth record (mainly by acquisitions) is outstanding and has shown an annual compounded growth rate of 16.6 percent over the past fifteen years. However, his net profit has grown at an annual compounded rate of only 14.5 percent! Because we may assume that profit is directly related to the ratio of effective to supportive personnel, then we may apply the Law of the Sphere just as well to the ratio between profit and sales[15] volume, as long as the relationship between sales and the number

---

14 I consider sixty-five effective employees out of a total of 100 to be an optimal number for a manufacturing plant.

of effective workers (in other words, the productivity of the workers) remains constant.

Let's examine the facts as stated in the company's annual report for 1997. In figure 2-4, I have plotted net profit versus annual sales. As you can see, the numbers conform well to the general trend predicted by the Law of the Sphere: 1997 profit = 1982 profit[16] × (Sales 1997/Sales 1982)$^{2/3}$. I can well sympathize with this CEO's frustration. The percentage of profit keeps slipping despite his best efforts—little does he realize that he is up against a natural law! While his aim is to reach a sales volume of $1 billion before the end of the second millennium (up from the present $720 million), he may only reach a net profit of 6.5 percent of sales as compared to the present 7.2 percent, following the dictates of this law—unless, of course, the IRS changes his tax bracket.

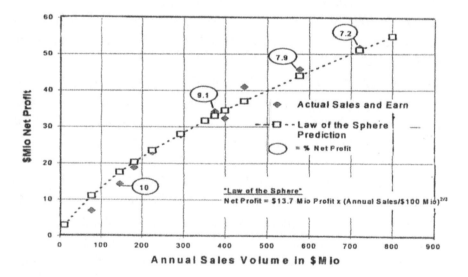

Figure 2-4

---

15 This, of course, implies that the number of supportive personnel increases exponentially in respect to sales volume.

16 Increased to fit curve averages.

Figure 2-4 shows the sales volume and profit before tax of a manufacturing company listed on the New York Stock Exchange. Note that the profits as a percentage of sales have declined with company growth, even though the overall profits have increased. This indicates a decrease in efficiency. This example shows that in the absence of knowledge about the precise numbers of supportive and effective personnel, the sales-to-profit relationship as described by the Law of the Sphere may be used as an analytical tool.

Unfortunately, it is nearly impossible to find accurate published reports on the ratio between effective and supportive personnel. We do, however, find published data regarding the relation-ship between firms' profits (either as a total sum or as a percentage of sales) and their total employment figures.

With few exceptions, a company's profits are always low if its total employment is too high. In other words, unprofitable companies employ more people than are required to provide goods or services at competitive prices. Exceptions arise when, for example, a company rents expensive office space or its business is based on importing hardware or material from a country whose currency has appreciated substantially against the U.S. dollar. Nevertheless, these exceptions should not distract us from the overall relationship between the number of employees and profit. Such a relationship can reflect the otherwise invisible ratio between effective and supportive personnel.

In my experience, it is very rare for the number of hours taken by an effective person to produce a certain part to vary between a small company and a large one. Such invariability, at least in the manufacturing sector, is dictated by the use of machine tools, which are all run automatically and at optimum speed.

Hence, we must conclude that the *only* reason why profit decreases in larger organizations is that the number of supportive personnel increases out of proportion to the necessary increase in the number of effective personnel. This becomes apparent when we analyze the dollar sales per person per year[17] versus the size of the company as expressed by its total

---

17 Defined as a company's yearly sales volume in U.S. dollars divided by the average number of that company's total employees.

number of employees. Figure 2-5 shows such a relationship. While there is quite a scattering of available data from manufacturing companies[18], the trend is unmistakable. Again, the sales volume per employee decreases drastically (as thereby do the companies' profits) with the increase in the size of a company or division as expressed by its number of employees.

Again, the Law of the Sphere can be used as a tool to explain and predict this trend.

A word of caution: exponential curves or equations cannot be extended *ad infinitum*. Reasonable benchmarks should be set for each individual case.

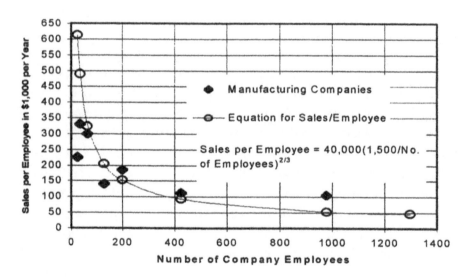

Figure 2-5

The projected value of $386,000 per fifty employees (in 1997 dollars) in figure 2-5 (solid line) may already be too high (except in refineries, power plants, chemical plants, or similar industries), because such a limit is set by the physical capacity of an individual worker or his or her machine

---

18 This might in part be due to some uncertainty as to which category (vertically or horizontally structured) a company belongs.

tool. On the other side of the spectrum, there may not be any company with sales of less than $70,000 per employee. If such a company *has* existed, it is probably bankrupt now. Another reason why we have companies still in business with very low sales per employee (see the entry in figure 2-5 for 1,000 employees) is that such a company may be located in a low-wage area of the United Sates or have plants abroad, where average yearly wages might be per-haps $25,000 per employee instead of $50,000 in high-cost areas. This would distort the statistics accordingly.

As in nature, nothing in business is exactly predictable. On the other hand, nothing in nature follows a linear relationship and, as the graphs in this chapter clearly show, neither is the relationship linear between company size (number of employees) and profit. The reader may argue that the Law of the Sphere is not applicable in all cases, and he is right. But even the most skeptical reader should admit that an exponential relationship does seem to exist. If he concedes this, then we can only argue about the numerical value (or values) of the exponential factors in our equation.

Remember, all our effort in controlling human economic endeavor is really an attempt to understand and to control chaos.

How to Reverse the Process

Any good manager who has inherited a large company may ask himself or herself whether the process of exponential administrative growth can be reversed. The answer is, probably not. One could consider splitting the company into two or three parts (if this is possible within the given product structure). This is called a *de-merger,* and is a ploy exercised not so much to gain efficiency (which it does not do—see the explanation below), but to gamble that the stock market value of each of the individual new divisions, when combined, will exceed the stock value of the old parent company.

Why does a de-merger not improve efficiency? Let's assume that you split a company with two independently run divisions, each of which has an 8 percent after-tax profit, in half. There is no reason to expect that the profit of either of these divisions will increase dramatically after the split-up. For an explanation, let's consult the Law of the Sphere. If you divide a large sphere (the parent company) into two equal halves, you still have the same ratio between effective and total personnel (the ratio between the curved surface area and the volume). For example, Company A has 10,000 employees. According to the 2/3 Law of the Sphere (see table 2-1), it has about 2,200 effective employees (using 100 as the base level) and 7,800 supportive employees, or a ratio of about 3.5 supportive to 1 effective. If you split Company A into two equal parts—Companies B and C—then each of B and C has 3,900 supportive and 1,100 effective personnel—still a ratio of 3.5 to 1!

In contrast, if B and C had grown independently from humble beginnings and as two separate companies to a total of 5,000 employees each, they each would have had 3,643 supportive and 1,357 effective personnel, for a ratio of only 2.7 to 1. This would have improved their productivity and, therefore, their before-tax profit by $[(1357 / 1100) \times 100]$ - $100 = 23$ percent. Alas, you can never turn back the clock. So, what are our real choices?

Well, one way to keep growing efficiently while at the same time improving your bottom line is to grow *sideways*. This can be accomplished by buying one or more smaller competitors, preferably in the $50 million or under sales range (that is, before they too become "waterlogged.") The trick here is to allow them to maintain their independence. The temptation is usually too irresistible for the staff people of the larger parent company (the buyer) to impose their own "goodwill" onto the unfettered hierarchy of the smaller purchased company. Such impositions start with the most innocent requests for a uniform financial reporting system (with the resultant need for a brand new computer system for the company being taken over) and inexorably lead to altering environmental regulations, overhauling patent systems, combining purchasing efforts, prescribing engineering and drafting practices, and exerting more hurtful pressures on inventory levels. All this is usually done behind the back of the CEO of the parent company, who is usually quite a common-sense type of a person, or so we would hope.

The requests begin quite innocuously, starting with a simple e-mail message from corporate headquarters. How long can the new general manager (usually an up-and-coming executive from the parent company) refuse such requests? Usually not for very long, if he still wants to be considered a "team player!" Such interference by his own staff into the affairs of an acquired firm must be strongly opposed by the parent company's CEO. This should be an ironclad rule.

Another rule should be to limit the growth of the acquired company to a manageable level and then start a new practical company, typically by splitting up parts of the product lines of the original company. What the CEO should do is clone—and, upon further growth, keep on cloning—the well-run new division.

The following is an example of how a small, acquired company with, say, 100 people, of whom 60 are effective and 40 are supportive, can grow. Assume further that the company has $25 million in yearly sales. Expenses are: 32 percent of sales for labor (salary and wages), 20 percent for material, and 20 percent for other expenses. This leaves a before-tax profit of 28 percent, or $7 million. Now, let's look at two different approaches to growth. Assume that the acquiring corporation is well-run and falls into the *excellent* category, where the number of effective personnel grows by a factor of 0.875 (according to the modified spherical law), or $X = Y(B/A)^{7/8}$, where X is the number of effective employees and B is the total number of employees. Assume further that the labor efficiency and the cost per employee ($80,000 per person) stay the same. The reference number A is 100 from above, and the number of effective employees (Y) is 60.

Table 2-3 shows the number of effective employees using the above equations, plus the resultant profit if the company keeps on growing as a single entity or subsidiary, ignoring any "economy of scale" effects.

One can clearly see what happens here. Despite a great and well-run central management team (7/8 factor), the percentage of profit degenerates steadily, and there will be a loss once employment exceeds 13,500. Incidentally, using an exponential factor of 2/3 (representing a true sphere) would result in the company already being in the red at only 3,000 employees!

Company Size	Yearly Sales	No. of Effective Personnel	No. of Support Personnel	Total Wages[c]	Material & Other	Profit	
(# of persons)[a]	($mio)[b]	"X"		($mio)	(40%)	($mio)	%
100	25	60	40	8	10.0	7	28
200	46	110	90	16	18.4	11.6	25
400	84	202	198	32	34	18	21
800	154	370	430	64	62	28	18
1600	282	679	921	128	113	41	15
3200	519	1245	1955	256	208	55	10
6400	951	2283	4117	512	380	59	6
12800	1745	4188	8612	1024	698	23	1.3

[a] Total employment
[b] $417,000 per effective employee
[c] $80,000 per employee

Table 2-3

Looking at the last line of the above table, we see that when the firm has 12,800 employees, it still makes $23 million in profit, even though the percentage on sales (the margin) is only 1.3. A stockholder would still be happy—after all, there is no loss. Yet he might have been happier if there had been two plants with 6,400 employees apiece and a profit of $59 million each. Such a cloning approach is explained on the following pages (see figure 2-6).

Original Plant	Total $ Sales	Profit $	Profit %	Total Effective Employ.	Total Employ.
[100]	25	7	28	60	100
[200]	46	11.6	25	110	200
[100] [200] [100]	96	25.6	27	230	400
[200] [200] [200]	138	34.8	25	330	600
[100] [200] [200] [200] [100]	188	49	26	450	800

Figure 2-6

All sales and profit numbers are in $ millions. Numbers in brackets are total employees per plant.

This figure demonstrates how cloning a company can maintain high profitability while increasing sales volume. In this example, an initial plant with 100 employees evolves into five separate plants with a total of 800 employees.

In contrast to the "vertical" growth example illustrated in figure 2-6, let's assume that we will split up each subdivision once its employment figure exceeds 200 (we will call this the *cloning* approach).

As you can see from figure 2-6, when the overall employment reaches 800, we have five (or more) independent operating subdivisions with total sales of $188 million and a pretax operating profit of $49 million (26 percent). Contrast this with the single company with the same 800 people from table 2-2, with sales of $154 million and a profit before tax of only $28 million (18 percent)!

This may be an idealized case, as not all cloned divisions grow at the same rate. Nevertheless, it serves as a guide to approaching the challenge of staying efficient while growing. The ultimate success of this approach depends on grooming good general managers who are adept at understanding the philosophy of staying lean and who are willing to maintain the proven management organization and style of the originally cloned successful division.

CHAPTER

3

The Economy of Scale and How It Affects Business

The biggest firm is not always the most profitable one.

The general consensus in the business world, supported by such renowned managerial consult-ants as Dr. Peter Drucker, is that the bigger the company gets, the more efficient it is. This belief is based on the following assumptions:

a. There is greater accessibility to capital, either through better access to capital markets or from the banks.

b. Increased quantity of purchased material will result in bigger discounts, and hence lower cost.

c. Pooling research and development will reduce R&D expenses.

d. Increased sales will get you market dominance, and hence reduce competition and raise prices for your goods.

e. Higher revenues will allow a greater advertising budget, hence creating better customer awareness of your business.

f. You will attract more talented managers.

All these are very valid arguments. Then why do companies begin to fail when they exceed a certain size? Well, as the German poet J. W. Goethe once said, "The good Lord makes sure that the trees do not grow into heaven." There are always absolute limits to growth. In trees, the height limit is reached when the tree loses the ability to pump its sap up the trunk. In animals, the size limit is achieved when it takes more energy to walk and forage than is provided for by the food it is able to eat. For that reason, the elephant is about the maximum size a land animal can get.

In companies, the limit of growth is reached when it costs more money to administer the organization than is accumulated through the production and sale of goods. This typically happens when there are too many organizational layers (reporting levels) and when the ratio of office workers to blue-collar workers exceeds a critical number. The U.S. auto industry is a prime example of this ratio in action (see chapter 8).

As shown in the assumptions listed earlier, there are very positive results derived from increasing the size of a company. This is called the economy of scale. The negative effects of growth include the unavoidable increase in the number of reporting layers and the associated number of office workers, who have a growth rate exceeding that of their blue-collar brethren. I call this the growth in overhead.

The following graph will show how this works. As seen in figure 3-1, the positive effects from the economy of scale produce a rapid increase in profit following increases in sales. How-ever, this is dampened by the left curve, representing the negative effects of growth in overhead. While relatively mild for low sales volume (typically for small companies), there is accelerated growth when sales volume increases—in other words, when companies grow.

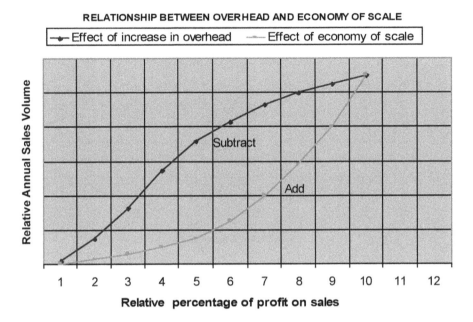

Figure 3-1

Figure 3-1 shows that at a given maximum sales volume, the economy of scale will result in 9.5 percent net profit. However, this is reduced by the same 9.5 percent loss resulting from the increase in overhead expenses; hence we have a 0 percent overall profit. On the other hand, at 50 percent of given sales, we have a 7.5 percent benefit and only 3.8 percent to deduct due to overhead. The result is a 3.7 percent net profit on sales. (Note that this is an arbitrary case and certainly not typical.)

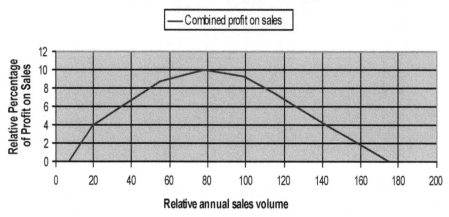

Figure 3-2

What we have to do now is combine these two effects—subtract the overhead numbers from the economy of scale numbers. This is shown in figure 3-2. On the left-hand side of the graph, we can see that the economy of scale effects predominate and profits go up rapidly, up to an assumed sales volume of about 78 (note that this is an arbitrary scale). Thereafter, the effect of the growth in overhead takes over and the curve reverses until eventually there is no more profit. The tree can grow no more![1]

---

1 Fred R. Kaen and Hans D. Baumann. "Firm Size, Employees and Profitability in U.S. Manufacturing Industries," SSRN Web site. Social Science Research Network. 1-13-2003

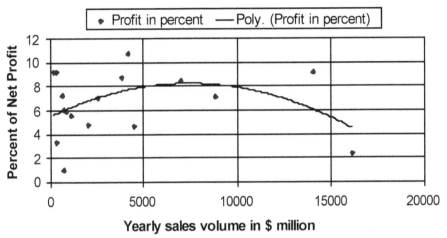

Figure 3-3

Figure 3-3 shows how this works in praxis.[2] Here I have plotted the results of well-known companies listed on the New York Stock Exchange, together with their percentage of net operating profit. As you can see, the trend curve representing average values resembles the theoretical curve from figure 3-2. Here the profit does not start at zero, because none of the listed companies had a low enough sales volume.

While there is a scattering of data—as one would expect due to the great diversity in individual company makeup—the graph clearly shows the reversing trend previously discussed. For this particular industry, the optimum sales volume seems to be $5 billion per year. The preferred way to grow from there on is to start a separate division.

---

2 Data from the General Electric Company was omitted because the majority of their profits were derived from insurance and leasing activities.

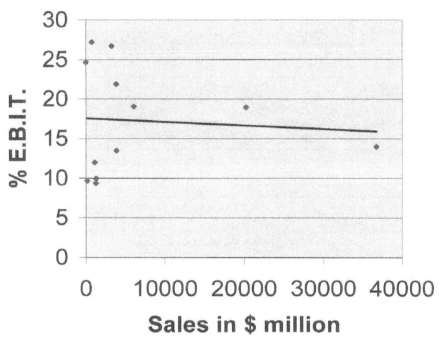

Figure 3-4

There are, of course, industries in which it is not possible to produce goods on a small scale. Chemical industries and refineries are cases in point. Figure 3-4 shows data from 1995 for the U.S. chemical industry. Here all companies are profitable, while profit deteriorates somewhat with size, at revenues exceeding $30 billion in sales per year. Here we see no effect of the economy of scale, nor of overhead. The reason is that the dollar sales per employee are very high, because goods are produced in bulk by very large equipment requiring very little manual labor. Take Dow Chemical Co. as an example. In the 2006 business year, this company had $49.1 billion in worldwide sales, yet employed only 42,578 people. This accounted for a yearly sales volume per employee of $1.153 million. The company's administrative and sales expenses were $1.660 billion, or 3.38 percent of sales. Now, a reduction in overhead of 10 percent would only affect the bottom line by 0.3 percent, which is well within the accounting system's margin of error. Contrast this with Emerson Electric Co., a typical manufacturing company. Its sales per employee during the same time frame were only $157,535, and its general administrative and sales (GA&S) expenses were 21 percent of sales, which is typical for that industry. Now, if Emerson were to accomplish a 10 percent reduction in overhead (GAS), it would be able to increase its profit by 2 percent—a significant savings!

While there is substantial scatter in the above graph, indicating that there are well-run as well as struggling companies, as there are in every business, there nevertheless is a discern able trend towards lower profits with increased sales volume. Still, each of these companies is profitable.

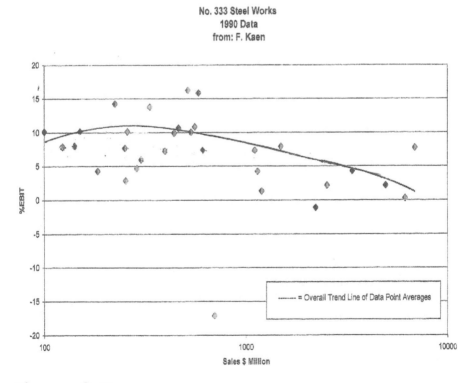

No. 333 Steel Works
1990 Data
from: F. Kaen

Figure 3-7

Figure 3-7 shows another example of the conflicting trends between economy of scale and increase in overhead. The optimum earnings in this particular industry seem to be a yearly sales volume of about $700 million.

Yet steel-rolling mills, on the other hand, are very demanding of capital. Between capital expenditure for high-cost machinery, depreciation, maintenance cost, and material, the cost of salaries and wages becomes a minor factor. This is evidenced by the very high sales per employee, as shown in figure 3-8.

Still, as the data reveal, fewer employees—that is, more sales per employee—will in-crease profit.

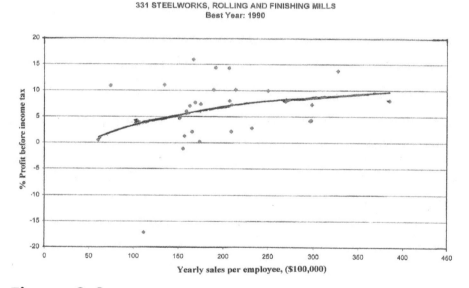

Figure 3-8

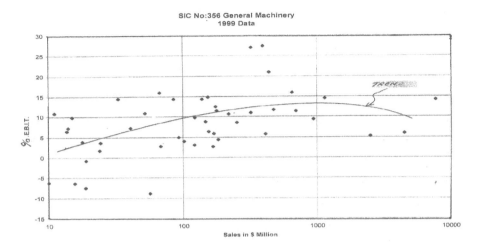

Figure 3-9

Figure 3-9 shows the 1999 data for forty-five companies classified as "general machinery" under SIC code 356, the government classification code for this specific industry. Here again we see our classic curve reversal, with small companies with around $20 million in yearly sales averaging only 5 percent profit before taxes. The highest profitability, at 27.5 percent, is reached at about a $300 million sales volume. The trend in profit increase (economy of scale) reverses above $1 billion in sales—in other words, when employment exceeds 5,000 (including six reporting layers and about 480 managers; see chapter 4).

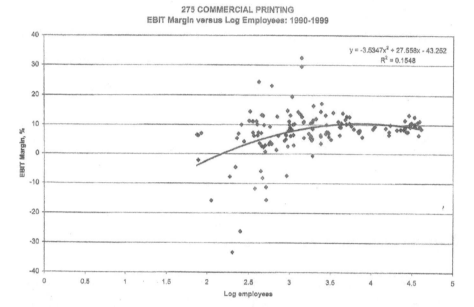

275 COMMERCIAL PRINTING
EBIT Margin versus Log Employees: 1990-1999

$y = -3.5347x^2 + 27.558x - 43.252$
$R^2 = 0.1548$

Figure 3-10

Commercial printing (SIC 2751), shown in figure 3-10, is a very competitive business. Here firms having only about two hundred employees are seen to fare badly, and some have losses of up to 32 percent. The break-even point is generally only breached when the level of employment exceeds 200 persons, with some companies attaining profits of 30 and 32 percent with about 2,000 employees. However, profit begins to decline again when employment exceeds 6,000—close to the data in figures 3-3 and 3-5.

As a final example, businesses involved with photographic equipment and supplies, as a whole, exhibit the trend reversal in earnings, as demonstrated in figure 3-11. While there is a marked variation in the individual business efficiency of smaller firms having yearly sales between $10 million and $15 million (their profits vary from -6 percent to +20 percent), a more uniform pattern emerges when sales exceed the billion-dollar mark.

One wonders whether this has more to do with market dominance due to size than to better business acumen.

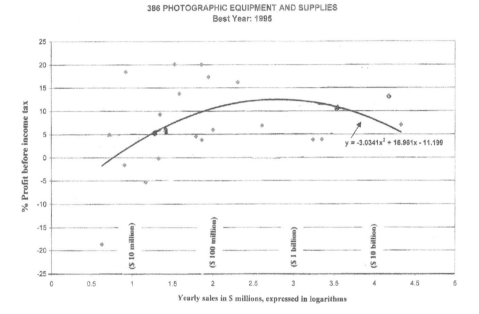

Figure 3-11

(All data in this chapter, unless otherwise indicated, are taken from: Fred R. Kaen and Hans D. Baumann, "Firm Size, Employees and Profitability in U.S. Manufacturing Industries," SSRN Web site, Social Science Research Network. January, 2003.)

CHAPTER

4

Reporting Layers—A Detriment to Efficiency

It may be fun, but not necessarily efficient, to have many people reporting to you.

Why do I say this? Communication between humans can be imprecise even on a one-to-one basis. So when information, orders, or instructions are passed from one person to another along a chain of command, we can experience serious problems. We all know how rumors can get distorted or exaggerated after passing from one family member to another. In companies, things can get worse, because information or orders can be modified, or even disregarded, by certain managers who have a selfish stake, pro or con, in the matter.

Even U.S. presidents are not immune to such problems. A case in point involved President John F. Kennedy. While traveling on an interstate highway near Washington, he spotted a large road sign pointing the way to CIA headquarters in Langley, VA. This upset him, as the CIA's location was supposed to be a secret. At the next cabinet meeting, he asked his secretary of the interior to have the sign removed. A few months later, the president spotted the sign again and summoned the secretary for an explanation. This good man replied, "But Mr. President, I immediately passed your request on to my assistant!" When the president saw the sign for the third time, he grabbed his car phone and called the road supervisor in charge of the highway. "Go out there and remove the sign," he said, "or I'll have you fired!" And you can believe that it was done!

We know of famous generals like Erwin Rommel who, frustrated by the chain of command, rode in a car to the front line in times of a crisis and issued commands directly to company commanders.

Most of us already know that the greater the distance between the office of a company's president and the assembly line, the fewer factual messages get passed down. The reverse is also true, as the president is typically carefully screened from bad news such as customer complaints or labor problems. This, of course, stems from managers' instincts of self-preservation. All this points toward a direct correlation between communication problems and the number of reporting layers.

So what can be done about it? Well, the best solution is to put a moratorium on or, better yet, reduce the number of reporting layers in your organization. First, let's study the relation-ship between the number of people in an organization and the resultant quantity of reporting layers.

Unfortunately, such data is hard to come by from industry, and I had to rely in part on my own experience. After all, no company's annual report publishes such data. However, the U.S. Army, being close in its organization to an industrial enterprise, can supply such data.

As of 2004, the U.S. Army had 500,203 active personnel.[1] Not counting the Secretary of the Army, his assistant secretary, the Joint Chiefs of Staff, the heads of the area command centers, and so on, the operational part of the army has eleven reporting layers starting at the squad level (led by a sergeant) and ending at an army group (led by a four-star general).

---

1 Wikipedia.org/wiki/Military of the United States. 1-2007

The following graph displays the number of troops in each unit (squad, platoon, company, etc.) up to the eleventh layer, where each unit represents a separate reporting layer. Be-cause the size of each group varies somewhat (there is a difference, for example, between infantry and artillery units), I used average numbers. However, this has little impact on the overall analysis. The next step was to derive an equation in order to make this relationship transferable to the industrial and com-mercial sectors. Here is such an equation:

$$N = [\log_{10} (\text{Number of troops or employees})]^{1.39}$$

where N is the number of layers for a given troop (or department) level. For example, the reporting layer for a division (15,000 troops) is: $N = (4.176)^{1.39} = 7.29$, where $4.176 = 10\log (15,000)$ or, rounded, the seventh reporting layer. As the graph in figure 4-1 shows, there is good overall agreement between the above estimating method and the actual data.

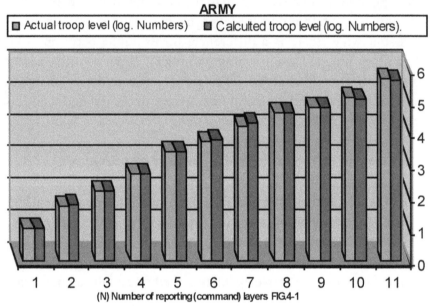

(N) Number of reporting (command) layers FIG.4-1

Figure 4-1

Figure 4-1[2] shows troop levels starting with a group of ten soldiers (a squad commanded by a sergeant) and ending at level eleven with 500,000 troops (an army groups commanded by a four-star general), and their respective command levels. We can see that the differences between the numbers estimated using the above equation and the actual numbers are quite small. This indicates that the equation is reasonably accurate. The U.S. Army, therefore, is a prime example of a vertically structured organization.

The US military also provides a prime example of why "small is beautiful." In short, smaller units are much more efficient than larger ones. We can see this in the percentages of officers serving in a particu-

---

2 Logarithmic numbers are used when numeric values exceed over several orders of magnitude. For example a log . number of 1 = 10 while a log. number of 6 = 10^6 = 1,000,000.

lar branch of the armed forces. I believe that nobody would argue that having more officers in a given unit will increase its fighting efficiency. Incidentally, according to the November 3, 2003 issue of *Barron's*, in 1941, there were only seven officers per 100 troops. This has swelled to nineteen officers per 100 soldiers in 2001. Inflation is everywhere!

Here is a breakdown for the year 2004:

Branch: Number of personnel: Percentage of officers

Army	Navy	Air Force	Marine Corps
500,203	375,521	358,612	180,000
13.9%	14.8%	20.4%	10.58%

Table 4-1

As we can see, the marine corps, the smallest branch, seems to be the most efficient fighting force.

Nevertheless, using the army again as a guide, we can now make an estimate of how many managers (in contrast to officers) are typically employed in a civilian organization. Using the 13.9%, or 69,307 officers out of 500,203 army personnel from above as a base level, we can now devise an equation to predict the percentage of officers (or, managers) for each reporting layer: Here I propose:

$$\text{Percent of officers or managers} = 12\log_{10}(N) + 1$$

Here are some calculated numbers:

N	E	%M	M*
1	10	1	1
2	50	4.6	3
3	150	6.7	10
4	600	8.2	43
5	1,500	9.38	140
6	5,000	10.3	520
7	12,000	11.14	1,330
8	30,000	11.83	3,550
9	80,000	12.45	10,000
10	180,000	13.1	23,800
11	500,200	13.9	69,300

E = number of troops or employees (rounded). N = number of given reporting layer. M = number of mangers or officers per reporting layer (rounded).

Table 4-2

Using the above numbers, we can estimate the number of officers in a company (the third layer) as 4.83 percent of 150 = 7.24 officers or, when rounded, seven. A brigade (the sixth layer), in contrast, has 10.3

* The commander of a squad is a sergeant, technically not an officer, yet the equivalent of a manager.

percent of 5,000 personnel, or 520 officers. Here we can see the striking decrease in the number of effective fighting troops when we get to larger units.

Figure 4-2 shows the geometric increase in managerial personnel in a more dramatic fashion. Here I plotted the number of managers/ officers against each number of successive reporting layers, as shown in table 4-2.

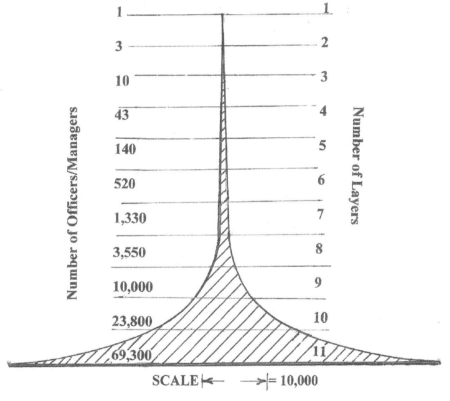

Figure 4-2

You may say that this is all well and good for the army, but it may not necessarily apply to private businesses. You are of course correct, because no two companies are alike in their organizational structure, and so there are wide variations in their respective numbers of managers. Nevertheless, what is important is that this matrix clearly shows that *the larger an organization gets, the greater the number of managers per capita.* It is therefore a good tool to explain the causes for the detrimental effects on efficiency of operation, and therefore on profit. Such views are shared by others. For example, Alan B. Krueger stated in the *New York Times* on February 6, 2003, in a discussion of the effects of military manpower in battle, "As in many industries, how-ever, there are *declining marginal returns* from manpower." (Emphasis in the original).

I can attest from my own experience that the estimated percentages shown in the above tabulation seem to apply reasonably well to at least two examples taken from industry. In a smaller company with eighty employees, there were eight managers, or 10 percent of the total workforce. On the other hand, a somewhat larger company with 1,200 employees had 212 managers, or 17.6 percent of all employees. These percentages exceed those given for the army. This is due to the fact that even small companies need a minimum number of departments such as sales, purchasing, production, and so on. We nevertheless here still see the trend of exponential growth in the number of mangers, and therefore overhead.

It may also be instructive to look at other governmental organizations, such as the famous FBI. In its pre-2002 structure, it had about 27,000 employees, yet nine reporting layers (one more than the army). It is not surprising, therefore, that there were serious communication problems between its field offices and its top brass in relation to the 9/11 attacks. But instead of creating smaller and more effective "anti-terrorist" organizations in response to the 9/11 attack, the U.S. government decided to create a single super-bureaucracy—the Department of Homeland Security. In addition, the president created a super-intelligence agency called the Office of the Director of National Intelligence. Now, you and I would think that the most important people reporting to this "intelligence czar" would be the director of the CIA, the head of intelligence for the defense department, and all the other intelligence chiefs. Sadly, we would be wrong. Here are the titles of the actual reporting positions[3]: the Chief Liberties Protection Officer, the CEO and Diversity Officer, the General Counsel, the Inspector General, the Chief Financial Officer, the Chief Information Officer, the Chief Human Capital Officer, and finally—perhaps as an after-thought—the Director of Intelligence Staff. Still, there seems to be something missing—how about the Chief Congressional Liaison Officer? Sad, isn't it?

Organizational sociologist Charles Perrow, in his book *The Next Catastrophe*,[4] suggests that, as a result of such runaway bureaucracy, "institutional failures are unavoidable." His solution is to decentralize, diversify, and build redundancy into all systems, and he concludes that "given the limited success we can expect from organizational, executive, and regulatory reform, we attend to reducing the damage that organizations can do by reducing their size." I can only agree wholeheartedly.

What does all this mean in terms of the organization of a company? Let's consider the case of two companies. Company A started as a small unit with only 200 employees. It grew rapidly to 600, then to 1,800, and finally to 5,400 employees by constantly enlarging its plant. It wound up with six reporting layers in a vertical structure with about 10.3 percent of 5,400 = 556 managers, according to the above estimate.

Now let's consider Competitor B's business (see figure 4-3 below). He also started with 200 employees. Next, he bought two other businesses, each with 200 employees. All of these businesses had to report to his original office. He expanded his business in due course, but instead of enlarging his original plant, he built additional and separate plants, each with 300 and later 600 employees. Each of his new plants had a general manager who was responsible for the profit and loss of his plant and who reported directly to the owner, who was still running his original plant. This then resulted in only four reporting layers in a horizontally structured business model. Now, let's see ... Company B

---

3 Wikipedia 9-23-07
4 Charles Perrow, *THE NEXT CATASTROPHE: Reducing our Vulnerability to Natural, Industrial, and Terrorist Disasters,* Princeton University Press, 2007.

wound up with the same number of employees as Company A—5,400—but with only four reporting layers, the owner of Company B employed only 8.2 percent of 5,400 = 443 managers. In other words, he had 21 percent fewer managers than his competitor. What an improvement in efficiency, and what savings in his payroll!

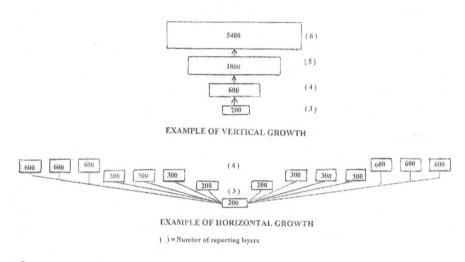

EXAMPLE OF VERTICAL GROWTH

EXAMPLE OF HORIZONTAL GROWTH

( ) = Number of reporting layers

Figure 4-3

One company that can serve as a role model for successfully integrated horizontal organization is Illinois Tool Works, Inc. At last count, this company had more than 600 independently operating divisions.

FINANCIAL RESULTS OF ILLINOIS TOOL WORKS, INC.

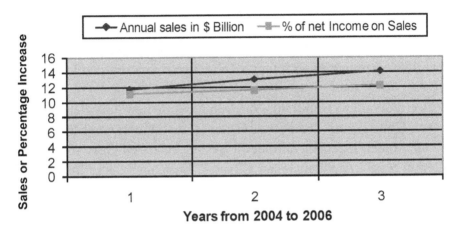

Figure 4-4

Each of ITW's many divisions has its own sales, accounting, human relations, and other typical departments. In addition, ITW allows each division to compete against another of its divisions if they happen to share the same marketplace—a practice so unusual in the business world that it seems almost to be breaking a taboo! The company's diverse products include cranks for car windows, welding equipment, and plastic bottle caps. James Farrell, the chief executive of ITW, is quoted as saying, "I split up units once they reach $50 million in sales." Such a unit would have about 200 employees and three reporting layers. No wonder this company is quite profitable and, as a result, demands a premium on the stock market. Figure 4-4 shows its sales and earnings for a three-year period. As you can see, there has not only been a constant increase in sales, but—what I consider more important—*a constant increase in the percentage of profit on sales.*

ITW's 2006 operating margins were 16.54 percent, as compared to only 9.56 percent for the industry as a whole.[5] Farrell expounded on his

---

5 finance.yahoo.com/q/co?=ITW , 8-2007

philosophy (which obviously matches mine), stating, "We believe that smaller is better to deal with. ... When you put two rather large things together, you create bureaucracy, which is very tough to overcome. Then you put systems in [place] to control the bureaucracy, and that adds more cost."[6] Indeed, fighting bureaucracy is one of major headaches for corporate management. To reduce it, or even just keep it from growing, is a nearly impossible task. As Farrell stated, companies try to hire efficiency consultants, or even create a new "efficiency department." However, all this accomplishes is to add more over-head.

One other argument advanced against unlimited firm size involves "control loss."[7] A phenomenon Oliver E. Williamson described in 1976, this involves the application of hierarchical organizations and what is also referred to as "serial reproduction effort" in transmitting messages or images between individuals. This brings about startling and radical alterations in the material dealt with—incidents and names are transposed, opinions and conclusions are reversed, and so on. Bartlett cited as an example a drawing of an owl that was redrawn by a succession of eighteen individuals. The final sketch always ended up looking like a cat!

To show the pervasiveness of excess overhead—and therefore reduced profitability—associated with company size throughout diverse industries, I will discuss some typical examples in the following chapters.

---

6 Chicago Tribune, 2-16-2002
7 Oliver E. Williamson and Scott E. Masten, Editors, *The Economics of Transaction Costs: An Elgar Critical Writing Reader* (Northampton, MA) p. 183.

CHAPTER

5

Mergers and Acquisitions

A merger of equals is never what it seems.

In any merger, despite pre-merger protestations, there are never any equals. Invariably, after about six months, there is a power struggle between the two company CEOs, with the weaker of the two departing. He will be solaced by being paid off with an umpteen-million-dollar "golden parachute." As in politics, there are no two equal rulers.

There are usually three reasons for companies to merge or to acquire typically smaller companies. First is a growth in sales volume of the company to be acquired. This impresses the shareholders and usually enhances the stock's value on Wall Street. Second, mergers improve the financial clout of a company when it comes to borrowing money or floating new stocks or bonds. One must be careful with acquisitions, because funds may have to be borrowed in order to finance them. The interest on these loans will depress a company's income, and the principal increases its liability, especially if the acquisition price was at a premium. Third—and this is seldom admitted—an acquisition or merger is often used to increase the market share of one's company in a given line of products. This can get dicey if one's market share gets too big, leading to a monopoly. Typically, the government's antitrust department will try to prevent this (unless one has good friends in Washington).

One should always beware, as a stockholder, when a merger of your company is contemplated. First, consider whether there is a true synergy—a potential for common cost sharing and resultant profit increase—or whether this is just a way to "grow" or provide "shareholder value." Such a move may mask an underlying actual decline in sales or profitability of your company. In that case, try to sell your company's shares as soon as you can. The bitter truth will emerge sooner or later. You are better off if you own stock in the company that gets acquired, the share price of which will typically soar, because the acquiring firm usually pays a premium. Even in this case, however, try to sell your stock, because the financial results of the combined companies will eventually suffer, for reasons explained in this book. Tyco Laboratories is a typical example, as is AOL.

When I was vice president of a larger firm, part of my job was to look out for suitable acquisition candidates. Invariably, I always discovered two problems, especially with smaller firms. The first is that when a company is very profitable, it is well-run, usually by an entrepreneurial individual managing a lean organization. Based on his profit level (maybe 30 percent before tax), he will demand a very high multiple to his company's book value or sales volume per year. For example, if profit B.I.T. is 30 percent of sales and the seller demands a price equivalent to 20 times earnings, this would be $20 \times 30/100 = 6$ times sales. This reduces the return on acquisition capital to 5 percent B.I.T. One solution to this dilemma is for the buyer to increase sales using the marketing power of his own organization.

However, there is a second problem—finding a suitable replacement for the (usually soon-departing) president of the acquired company. According to Mark Herndorn of Watson Wyatt Worldwide in Dallas, Texas, 47 percent of acquired executives leave in the first year and 73 percent of those remaining leave within the first three years. This leads to the buyer having the daunting task of finding a qualified person in his own organization. A less-qualified individual will surely increase bureaucracy and add inefficiency, as he will tend to simply follow the habits and customs of the parent company, which is typically much larger and less profitable. For more details, see the chapter on the Law of the Sphere.

Another problem I encountered—or, more accurately, the second type of seller I en-countered—was a not-so-well-run enterprise that was either close to bankruptcy or had marginal profit rates of 5 percent B.I.T. or less. The invariable reason for such a company's troubles was bad management. Again, the problem is how to find a suitable manager to run such a company after you buy it. Its selling price is usually book value or one times annual sales, which is not problematic, but reducing the number of redundant employees in such an inefficiently run company (the key to better profitability) certainly is.

Due diligence for marginally profitable companies is especially important. Some of the marginal profit may only exist in nonsellable inventory, for example. So, as paradoxical as it sounds, a cheap acquisition can cause major headaches, and so it is often better to pay a premium for a better company.

In the previous chapter, you learned that increasing a company's size eventually reduces the profit margin. This is true if a company grows as a monolithic entity, but not necessarily if it grows simply by adding a string of other semi-independent companies to its corporate corral. This is very similar to the cloning solution discussed in the Law of the Sphere chapter.

Consider the corporate umbrella as the thread through the string of pearls as shown in figure 1-2 in chapter 1. As in nature, each pearl has its own special size and luster. Consider each pearl as an individual, semi-independent division with its own size and profit level. It even helps to allow them to retain their previous company names and logos. As long as a division doesn't grow too fast and its product lines don't become obsolete, its profit will remain fairly constant, barring a recession or other major disruption.

The profits of the corporate parent—the owner of the string of pearls—simply reports the average profit of all those individual pearls (its divisions). The example in figure 1-2 shows a total of seventeen pearls or divisions having a total yearly sales volume of $1,581 million. Assume further that the average profit before tax is 16.5 percent. The president decides to buy another company that has a sales volume of $150 million per year at a rate of profit of 15.9 percent. This will increase parent company's next-year sales to 1,581 + 150 = $1731 million, and its overall rate of profit to [(0.165 ×1581) + (0.159 × 150)] / 173 = 0.164, or 16.4 percent.

Making another acquisition or merger (if skillfully done) will just add another pearl to the string. If the newest pearl is especially bright (a division with above-average earnings), then it will add to the overall luster of the strand as a whole—in other words, the corporate profit average will increase. This is good corporate strategy because by enlarging your corporation through mergers and acquisitions, you will show your shareholders a continuous increase in sales volume and profit. That the profit percentage stays fairly level, as explained previously, need not be advertised. What Wall Street is interested in is your price/earnings ratio. This is independent of the percentage of profit on sales. As long as you add one additional pearl to your string, your profit sum will go up, and so will your share price if the P/E ratio remains constant, unless you float more stock and dilute your earnings. For example, if your sales last year were $5 billion and your profit $500 million (a 10 percent profit), then, based on a P/E ratio of 20, your stock may be worth 20 times $500 million, or $10 billion (this is called market capitalization). This year, you buy a new company with $500 million in sales and a profit of $60 million (financed by loans). Now, your total sales have grown by 10 percent to $5.5 billion, and your profit has grown to $560 million (neglecting interest charges). This will now demand a new stock price of 20 times $560 million, or $11.2 billion. Note that your stock value has grown from $10 to $11.2 billion, a 12 percent increase, even though your percentage of profit only grew from 10 to 10.18 percent, or hardly at all. Overall, this is a good strategy, one that is employed by a number of successful companies, such as General Electric and Emerson Electric Co. Not surprisingly, it takes people with vision to run these companies—not to mention phenomenal memories to keep everything in focus!

Figure 1-3 in chapter 1 shows an impressive and consistent growth in both sales and total profit of one typical company that has a successful merger and acquisition strategy. However, a larger corporate umbrella does not guarantee a growth in percentage of profit. Figure 1-3 shows the rather impressive growth in total after-tax profit, which increased in the fifteen years between 1983 and 1998 from $330 to $1,229 million—a feat that would make the heart of any Wall Street analyst beat faster. However, if you analyze the percentage of profit before income tax (I use this measure because the effective tax rate decreased from 43.9 percent in 1983 to 36.1 percent in 1998), you will see, in figure 1-4, a decrease from 15.4 percent in 1983 to 14.3 percent in 1998. This is certainly not a ringing endorsement of the often-held theory that there is greater cost efficiency with an increase in size. Nevertheless, the management of this company did fairly well despite the almost fourfold growth in size during those fifteen years, realizing that each acquired subsidiary adds more complexity to the already barely manageable complex. The nagging question is: Would the overall profit level of the acquired companies have been higher if they had been left alone? We will never know the answer!

Luckily for the U.S. economy, the credit crunch at the beginning of 2008 put a temporary stop to a lot of merger and acquisition activities. As reported in the *Wall Street Journal* of January 8, 2008, the pending acquisition of PHH Corp. by Blackstone Group fell apart. Difficulties in getting financing also put the $19 billion buyout of Clear Channel Communication and the $33 billion deal for the Canadian telephone company BCE Inc. in jeopardy.

Now, on to the not-so-successful mergers and acquisitions.

Bad Mergers

According to Cornelius Grove & Associates LLC, as reported in the March 2000 issue of *Business NH Magazine*, mergers and acquisitions have an unfavorable impact on profitability and are strongly associated with lower productivity, labor unrest, high absenteeism, and poor accident rates. According to Mercer Management Consultants, Inc., and as reported in the same magazine, about 50 percent of all mergers fail to meet expectations.

So, let's start with leveraged buyouts. You may not want to read on if you are one of the few individuals who can pat their wallets with satisfaction because you owned shares in a company that was taken over at a grossly overpaid price. The story is less cheerful for those who held shares in the company that did the buying.

The mood of an acquired company's employees also tends not to be buoyant. Notice that whenever such a merger is announced, there is always talk of eliminating several thousand jobs to save umpteen million dollars. Luckily for those employees, this is mostly empty talk intended to impress Wall Street. Even if employees of the newly acquired company *are* laid off to save money, substantial sums are still spent on consultants who claim to be able to figure out how to make it all work.

As stated by David McCourt, the chairman of RCN, in the *New York Times* on August 27, 1998, "AT&T announces a takeover of TCT; Bell Atlantic, which is still adjusting to its acquisition of Nynex, merges with GTE; SBC Communication buys Pacific Telesis and then Ameritech. The list goes on and on, but these deals share one trait (beyond paying the greens fees of lawyers and investment bankers)—they probably won't work." All I can add to this is, "Amen!"

At this writing, there are intense negotiations underway concerning a possible merger between Delta and Northwest Airlines. Yet instead of possible reorganization plans and cost-cutting ideas (see chapter 9), the top item of discussion, according to the *WSJ*, has been how to allocate the managerial positions of the merged company among the top brass of the current companies. Absurd, isn't it?

Banks provide good examples of bad mergers. When two regional banks merge, they typically combine their headquarters staff, but close— you guessed it—their branch offices, which they replace with ATMs. The branch offices are the outer layer of the sphere representing the total company—they are where the daily business occurs and where the profit comes from. They are comparable to the sales departments of manufacturing companies. And yet, looking at the Law of the Sphere, this closure of bank offices seems pre programmed. Consider the case of two banks, A and B (figure 5-1), of equal size, having, say, 500 employees each, of which 250 work in branch offices (on the surface area of each sphere). After a merger of the two banks, the new *volume* of the sphere (the total employment of the company) is $2 \times 500 = 1{,}000$.

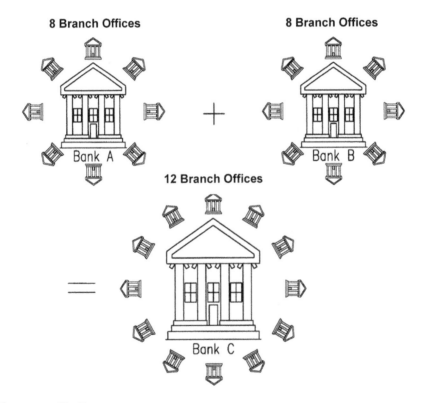

Figure 5-1

Example of the merger of two equal-sized banks. Per the Law of the Sphere, the new number of branches declines to 12.7.

Number after merger = $8 \times 2^{2/3} = 12.7$. This agrees with the graphic demonstration shown below.

The new surface area, according to our law, should now be $(1,000/500)^{2/3}$ $\times (250) = 397$. Because the old number of branch office employees was 2 $\times 250 = 500$ employees, the merged company has to lay off $500 - 397 = 103$ employees, or 10.3 percent of the total workforce. This is an accurate representation of what typically happens, as you well know from reading the local papers. Figure 5-1 shows the home office/branch office relationship in a simplified graphical form for easy understanding.

You start with two equal-sized banks A and B, each having eight branch offices. You now merge these two banks to create a new bank, C. This doubles the volume (total employment) of bank C over that of A or B. Now, the new bank's sphere must increase its diameter by about 1.26 times (because volume is a function of the cube of the diameter, $1.26 \times 1.26 \times 1.26 = 2$). We therefore draw a circle around bank C that is 26 percent larger than those around banks A or B.

Notice that we have space for only about twelve equally sized branch offices around the circumference of bank C, thus forcing a reduction from the overall pre-merger number of sixteen branches. To be exact, and using the Law of the Sphere, the new number of branch offices = old number per bank x (number of banks)$^{2/3}$, or NEW = 8 x $(2)^{2/3} = 12.7$ post-merger branches. This is a reduction of 20.6 percent! Most branch employees are people in the *effective* (i.e., profit-producing) category. Because 50 percent of all pre-merger employees worked in branch offices, the number of laid-off employees is 50 percent of 20.6 percent, or 10.3 percent, as explained previously.

A case in point is a news item that appeared in the April 3, 1999 issue of *The Economist*, which stated, "Bank One is to cut about 4,000 jobs, 4 percent of their work force, and take a $526 million charge in the aftermath of its $20.7 billion merger with First Chicago." This after Bank One already took a $984 million charge in the fourth quarter of 1998, making its total loss $1.51 billion, or 7.3 percent of the original purchase price, with probably more losses to come! One wonders where all that money could possibly go. I suspect that most of it went to attorneys and underwriters.

Returning to our hypothetical bank example, you may wonder what happens to the profit now that we have 103 fewer profit-producing or *effective* employees. Banks have to raise their fees to cover this deficiency in income. Looking at our bank statements, we are all aware of this trend. According to the *Palm Beach Post* of April 12, 1999, a Federal Reserve study showed that bigger banks, including those created by mergers, tend to charge higher fees than smaller ones. At commercial banks in 1998, net interest income totaled $174.5 billion, but fee income grew to $104.5 billion (a growth of 150 percent over the previous ten years, during which bank mergers accelerated). More specific examples were listed in the February 5, 2000 issue of *TIME* magazine:

BANK FEES:	Small Banks	Large Banks
Low-balance, non interest, check fees:	$5.62	$8.20
Stop payment order:	$13.92	$21.50
ATM withdrawals at other banks:	$1.09	$1.32

Although these are old numbers, the comparison is still valid.

An example of a bad merger that could not be cured by fee increases was that of R.J. Reynolds and Nabisco, the leveraged buyout that made history in 1985. The company has since split up after being saddled with high debt financed by junk bonds. Other companies were not so lucky. According to KDP Investment Advisors of Montpelier, Vermont[1] , of twenty-five cases between 1985 and 1989 in which companies were saddled with more than $1 billion in debt, almost half defaulted on their loans. Others filed for bankruptcy or had to sell off assets.

There are ample signs that mega-mergers don't work. Dupont split off its remaining 70 percent share of Conoco, Inc., and Hewlett-Packard

---

1 *New York Times*, March 14, 1999, p. 8

sold off a portion of its $7.6 billion-per-year business that produces test and measurement equipment, to cite only two cases.

The managerial complexity of big mergers can be mind-blowing. When Citibank merged with Travelers, the combined company had 150,000 different types of accounts (accounting ledgers), requiring twenty-eight different computer systems![2]

According to the June 5, 1999 issue of *The Economist*, due to mergers in the European insurance industry, the market share of the top five insurers in Britain had risen from 22 percent in 1990 to 36 percent in 1998, yet the overhead expenses as a percentage of premiums had gone up from 29 to 33 percent. This is not a ringing endorsement of *bigger is better* (see chapter 11).

As with all things in life, what goes up must come down. Merger mania creates firms so large that, absent monopolistic market dominance, their complexity and inefficiency will reach an unsustainable level, and, as a last resort, they will be forced to de-merge.

Remember that large corporations can only survive by being conglomerations of numerous quasi-autonomous divisions or subdivisions, or by starting up as separate divisions, such as the Cadillac division of General Motors. Bigness certainly has its price!

Demergers

There are more demergers than one might suspect. The reason is that less publicity is given to them, partly because companies are hesitant to admit that merging was a mistake in the first place. Another reason might be that such a de-merger is an act of desperation to rectify the foolishness of prior management.

Yet, even here, Wall Street and its PR men will try to make it an attractive deal for the shareholders by stating something to the effect that, "We discovered that the value of each of the to-be-demerged entities

---

2 Hans D. Baumann. *The Ideal of Enterprise.* (New York: Vantage Press, 2002).

is worth more than their present combined capitalized equity," conveniently forgetting that a few years back they claimed exactly the opposite in order to talk the stock up. Then they promised shareholders huge financial benefits due to synergism and resultant cost savings (which typically never materialized). The sad results quite often were a swollen bureaucracy and lower profits of the combined firm. Unfortunately, this only becomes apparent after a few years. The management responsible for the merger has by then safely departed after having received millions of dollars in bonuses or from their "golden parachutes."

On March 27, 2008, Motorola Inc. announced that it would split itself into two separate entities due to pressure from one of its major shareholders. Motorola's executives explained the move by saying, "This will allow the two companies to focus on their respective strengths and weaknesses." Mark Sue, an analyst for RBC Capital Markets, rightly responded by saying, "We are not convinced that splitting the organization ultimately enhances shareholder value." I certainly agree with his assessment.

There are, of course, other reasons for wanting to demerge a company. One might be to get rid of a money-losing division or subsidiary. American Express (which has had financially independent subsidiaries) is such an example, having divested itself of AMEX Life, Fireman's Fund, and Lehman Brothers, which resulted in a 100 percent increase in profits for the surviving parent company (see chapter 11).

However, the breakup of a fully integrated company is a near impossibility. How does one split up a manufacturing plant housed under one roof? This was exactly the problem I once faced when a well-known aerospace company tried to sell a valve business housed in the same factory building used for the production of precision aircraft instrumentation. After studying the matter for some time, I finally gave up and walked away from the deal. Besides, as my readers know by now, the ratio between productive and total employees will not change if you split up a vertically integrated company (or a factory, for that matter). Hence, no financial benefits can be reaped through such a de-merger.

CHAPTER

6

---•--- --- ---•---

Meetings, or Managing by Committees

Committee decisions evolve generally around the arguments of the participant who has the greatest stamina, and are not necessarily based on the merits of the case.

It would be interesting to find out what people do in order to fill the time available during a good deal of their working hours. This quest brings to mind the old question asked in jest: "Are you an employee, or do you work here?" A couple of less-than-productive activities that come to mind are reading and writing e-mail messages and attending meetings. The latter can be the most harmful to businesses, as they not only take time away from more productive work, but they also mask the fact that a good portion of meeting attendees are redundant employees.

I therefore place special emphasis on company meetings, because they account for the lion's share of wasted manpower. Furthermore, I believe that the number of meetings in a company is directly related to the number of reporting layers in its organization.

What started this meeting craze? In the past, there were always meetings of some sort or another—board of directors meetings come to mind. However, these happened on relatively rare occasions, and the subjects discussed were usually important. This all changed after the 1980s. What was the reason? To paraphrase Professor Parkinson, "Meetings expand to fill the time available." Computerized offices and the associated reduction in time needed for "number crunching" released untold man-hours, which gradually became idle.

This pool of available and otherwise unused employee time evolved into a culture of meetings. I can attest to this development from my own experience as an engineer.

When I started out, we had to use a slide rule to calculate the equations needed to design our machinery. We had to look up the equations in handbooks and write the raw data on yellow notepads. All this took about six hours a day, on average. The balance of our time was taken up working in a laboratory, or even by occasionally reading a trade journal. Then, in the1970s, pocket calculators became available. Now we didn't have to worry about our decimal points. Logarithms and algebraic functions were all pre programmed. This cut time for calculations down to an average of four hours a day. Finally, in the 1980s and 1990s, personal computers appeared. Now all one had to do was input the design data. Everything, including the equations, was al-ready programmed. This part of the design process had now been cut down to two hours a day. The question then arose, "Because we employ the same number of engineers and design the same number of widgets, what happened to the four hours per man that were saved?" A very good question! My answer is that about half of the idle time is spent in meetings, and the balance in answering and writing e-mail messages. This explains why, despite this massive addition of tech-

---

1 As pointed out by Stephen Roach, a Morgan Stanley analyst, there is no evidence that computers actually save labor, taking the economy as a whole. He states that the productivity gains of the information age are just a myth. New Hampshire Sunday News, 8-17-01997.

nology in the workplace, there seems to be no reduction in the number of employees.[1] Here is a little anecdote e-mailed to me by a friend:

> *His relatively small company had a problem. They had seventy-seven employees, of which forty-two worked in the office looking for ways to call for meetings. The problem was that the company only had five conference rooms, which only allowed for two hundred hours of conference time a week. All were fully booked. The solution: new "online conference room reservation software." Now everyone could be properly scheduled for his or her time in one of the five conference rooms to discuss what else but "how to increase productivity and cost containment!"*

Incidentally, this happened after the company had moved from a smaller building into a larger facility. Sadly, the old building had only had one conference room. However, there was some compensation for this lack of meeting space—the profit of the company had been much higher! The best solution to a lack of meeting space is to hire fewer office employees.

We seem to be unable to conduct any business at all nowadays without having a meeting. These could range from a casual encounter at the water cooler to a friendly business lunch. The latter was my favorite, because it combined the necessary with the pleasant. Another advantage of the business lunch is that it establishes a tight time-frame for the discussion. Finally, it puts the participants more at ease. (Who wants to argue on a full stomach?)

In the business world, there are two basic types of meetings:

1. The meeting to inform or instruct. This could involve a group of students getting trained, salesmen being taught the merits of a new gadget to be manufactured, a traveling salesman explaining his wares, or the CEO telling his employees that their company has been profitable, to name a few examples.

2. The meeting to resolve issues, gain consensus, and make group decisions. This could involve something as harmless as deciding

on the color of the walls of the executive washroom, or something more relevant, such as the amount of alcohol to be added to a mouthwash product. Activities of standards-writing committees or boards of directors revolve around such meetings.

This second type of meeting has the biggest impact on how companies are run and, more importantly, on the bottom line. As mentioned before, in order for budding CEOs to advance through a company's hierarchy from relatively obscure positions, they have to rely more and more on the consensus formed in meetings by their department heads, who quite often rely in turn on a consensus-level input from their own subordinates. (This could lead to an absurd case in which the originator of a top-level company policy directive might be a lowly clerk who somehow missed his calling!)

Because group consensus is never created spontaneously, it can take many meetings for a decision to be made. This means that two extreme-polarity alternatives (one that may be truly innovative but risky and the other impractical or even absurd) are typically whittled down to something that everybody—or at least most members—can feel comfortable about. At about the fifth meeting, all but the most persistent advocate of a given issue give up (if for no other reason than sheer boredom), and finally everybody nods approvingly. Voila! Consensus is achieved.

We all know the adage, "A camel is a racehorse designed by committee." This is not always a laughing matter. I have known many companies where it is unheard of to have a product developed by a responsible individual engineer. The mildest rebuke he would get for trying would be to be admonished that he was not a "team player." The unavoidable consequence of such group design is at best a very mediocre product. One of the more sinister consequences of managing by committee is the subsequent total lack of individual responsibility for a bad policy decision. A committee is a faceless entity in which it can become all too easy to hide.

If we look back in history, we see that the bulk of innovations that made the United States a technical giant were made by creative individuals such as Alexander Graham Bell, Harvey Firestone, George Westinghouse, and Henry Ford, to name a few. Today, we have individual giants like Steve Jobs, who with Steve Wozniak developed the first personal computer, or Jeb Raskin, the developer of the Mac computer, or Tim Berners-Lee, who developed the World Wide Web. While Thomas Edison was a prolific inventor, he had his team of technicians. However, it was *he* who had the brilliant ideas, not his "team." They were employed to do the testing and what we might now call "product design."

Napoleon Hill, in the last century, thought that one could create a "mastermind" group, a creative team that could combine the brainpower of many individuals in order to enhance creativity. Unfortunately, such concepts do not work, as they counteract human nature. Besides, one cannot simply add a mass of brains together and hope that the outcome might be the brain of a genius.

There are, of course, projects that are too big or too multi disciplined for a single engineer, designer, or scientist to handle or understand. However, clear responsibility should be assigned to individual components or portions of such a project, and on these individuals the praise or blame should rest.

Meetings have evolved their own culture. There are meetings to plan meetings, meetings to discuss meetings, and don't forget meetings to establish rules for holding meetings. Here are a few names (just add the word *committee*) that most of us are already familiar with: budget, finance, marketing, cost reduction, loss prevention, compensation, safety, environmental, materials, procurement, security, technical steering, standards coordination, computer system, grievance, advisory, management, director—and my favorite, the joint safety, security, and loss prevention committee! Guess what this is: "The Furniture Commodity Strategy Team." Frankly, I don't know either, but I think it has to do with the recycling of used office furniture.

As you can see from the above sampling, there is no single business activity that is safe from our diligent meeting attendees. If we probe deeper, we find there is the dry-run or try-out meeting, especially prevalent when employees prepare for budget meetings. It seems that the sole purpose of such a meeting is to ensure that all the overheads are in the correct order and conform to the party line, and to rehearse the presentations to make sure that nothing embarrassing will ever be said in front of the president or the chairman of the board.

To define meetings for the purpose of this discussion, what I have in mind is not the chance encounter of two employees at the water cooler, nor the habitual meeting of elderly re-tired gentlemen at the park bench, but the organized get-together of colleagues at a defined location (Conference Room 435C), at a given time (8:30 am), and (one hopes) with a fixed agenda.

The typical day of a mid level manager might start with a 7:00 AM breakfast meeting with an out-of-town visitor, followed by the weekly operations meetings from 8:30 AM to 11:00 AM. At this time, he checks his e-mail messages that inform him of the meeting schedules for the coming month and specify his expected contributions. While reviewing his notes, checking his voice mail, and munching on his sandwich for lunch, he is interrupted and told that the scheduled marketing meeting has been rescheduled from 2:00 PM to 1:30 PM. This leaves him barely enough time to sort through his PowerPoints before dashing off.

The theme of this next meeting is not so much what the next product should be in order to help improve the company's sagging bottom line, but how to structure its presentation using the latest (thanks to highly paid consultants) pyramid scheme of "added value." This meeting finally comes to an end at 4:00 PM, after a very lively debate over the question of whether to use two or three parallel overhead projectors at the upcoming top management presentation. Three is the ultimate consensus, which leads to another intriguing question—which of the three projected texts should be read aloud?

Going back to his office, our manager realizes that he is late for his 4:00 PM appointment with an out-of-state visitor who, sure enough, is sitting patiently at his desk. Apologizing and trying frantically to remember the reason for this visit, he tries to overcome his embarrassment by starting a discussion about the latest winning streak of the local professional baseball team. This, if nothing else, will soon establish the needed camaraderie and spirit of teamwork between our hero and the out-of-towner. When the visitor finally leaves at 5:10 PM, it's time to prepare for the next day—that is, for the next day's meetings.

From outward appearances, this has been a very busy day. But there is a nagging question at the back of our minds: Was anything tangible actually accomplished? How were sales in-creased? How was the bottom line (the profit) improved? If it was, in some obscure way, it certainly wasn't measurable, and was probably out of proportion to the salary paid to our hero (which assumption he would certainly hotly deny).

Unfortunately, the above scenario is no exaggeration, but a daily ritual in our corporate structure. As a quite undesirable by-product, from a social to a health problem point of view, this meeting mania has gone to an extreme and spawned a middle-management habit of working an excessive amount of overtime, including weekends, which is mostly spent organizing and "digesting" meetings. How else can you finish the *productive* assignments you are committed to doing (and where else will you find the time to write your presentation paper for the next meeting)? While it seems paradoxical, it is not uncommon for middle-management employees to work fifty-five to sixty hours a week, not counting travel time.

Just to show to what extremes meetings can go, consider the following true story told to me by a very reliable but understandably unnamed source. A corporate budget review was scheduled for November 1. Frantic staff work began in July to prepare the necessary statistical and backup data. About four weeks later, all department managers were requested to incorporate the pro-posed budget figures into their respective department budgets with a detailed breakdown of the effects of various line items in the budget not only for the coming year, but also as regarded the next *five year plan.*

The end of August saw the first of five approximately day-and-a-half-long *rehearsal* meetings attended by twenty-six participants, each with an average of ten overhead graphs to present. Copies of these were neatly tacked along the wall of the oversized conference room for public review and comments by the "team." Anything not conforming to the *leitmotiv*, or graphs not presented in the shape of a pyramid, were rejected.

By October 15, after the last rehearsal—each of which, incidentally, always included reading all the fine text of each slide aloud—everything had fallen into place. Expected questions from the corporate CEO were posed, and acceptable answers were rehearsed by everyone (you never knew whom he might ask!) The divisional vice president sighed with relief, "We're ready!"

Then, the bombshell burst—the budget meeting was postponed to January 3. This caused a frantic redirection of effort—after all, there were now two more operating months to consider. Luckily, the bulk of the presentations could be salvaged; therefore, it was only necessary to hold four additional rehearsals before the big day.

Total *rehearsal* costs alone for the 2,800 man-hours expended by the meeting attendees translated into about $175,000 in salaries, to which should be added at least $100,000 in staff work and travel expenses.

Of course, one should not overlook the very positive human aspects of meetings. Psychologically, meetings satisfy our herd instinct—the need to belong to and interact with a group of our peers. This need becomes more and more important when increasing numbers of office employees are penned in cubicles or spend lonely hours in front of computer screens without any face-to-face human interaction. We all have a need for *belonging* that must be satisfied in any healthy office environment. It is a worthy challenge for a good manager to provide effective ways for employees to come together to satisfy this emotional yearning, while avoiding repeatedly scheduled, time-wasting, and inefficient meeting rituals.

Also on the positive side of the meetings ledger, receiving an invitation to a meeting rein-forces one's feeling of belonging to a team. In fact, an occasional invitation to a meeting can be used as a reward for work performed well, as would be an in-between, or yearly, bonus, for example.

Being a regular invitee to a specific meeting, such as a weekly cost review, makes one a *de facto* team member. It reinforces our longing to be part of a select group, very much like that which our ancestors in the Stone Age felt when they hunted together, or, more recently, like that experienced by soldiers who fought together in an infantry squad. Group membership instills the satisfaction of belonging and the pleasure of camaraderie.

Still, keep meetings to an absolute minimum.

Electronic Conferencing

It should be very easy, in our electronic age, to have more virtual meetings, such as video conferences and the like. This would be especially cost-effective when a portion of the conferees are located overseas, and would result in tremendous savings in travel expenses. Furthermore, the time one would have spent traveling could be spent doing productive work.

However, despite all these impressive advantages, there is a certain reluctance to em-ploy electronic means of communication other than the telephone, fax, or e-mail. First of all, there are the time differences, especially between North America and Asia, which would mean that some of the conference participants would have to be awake and at their best at midnight, or even later. Second, a video conference does not allow for pre meeting personal interactions in which people can form a consensus or find allies in pursuit of a given agenda issue. Thirdly—and this is quite important—one is much less able to study the body language of the other participants, nor can one read the faces of the people in the room who might be out of focus of the camera. Annoying glitches like electronic noise and satellite-imposed time lag can also be quite detrimental. Finally, the camera itself is often poorly controlled. I once attended a video conference where the chairman of the board gave a speech. Initially, he sat behind a table, but during his presentation, he decided to get up. From then on, we watched his feet and legs for the re-minder of his talk, which was quite amusing for those who watched.

There is one aspect of video conferencing that makes it superior to in-person meetings: it is much better suited to teaching people how to sell a product or how to repair equipment, to mention two examples. It enables you to combine a video presentation with a telephone hookup for the creation of an interactive schoolroom environment.

What to do about meetings?

There are numerous ways to increase the efficiency of meetings, such as by shortening their duration and by running them in a more businesslike manner (having a good chairperson). According to Milo C. Frank,[2] "The difference between a stimulating discussion and a productive meeting is results!"

Of course, the best way to run meetings is to have none! The second-best way is to have as few as possible. Decisions should be made by a CEO or department head following input and/or advice from his or her subordinates, but *never* by a unanimous committee vote. This way, he or she can take full credit for a good decision or full blame for a bad one. This is the way it should be.

Why have I discussed meetings at such great length? Because in a corporate structure, they contribute more than anything else to the highly wasteful allocation and misuse of mostly salaried labor, and to bad business decisions. While decisions derived in committees create consensus (which may be positive), the consensus is only arrived at after considerable time—time that, in our ever-faster business cycles, has become a rare commodity. Most Japanese companies were once known to run their businesses by the consensus method. That is no longer true. More and more companies can no longer afford this luxury and have discarded this relic from the past. And never confuse meeting-derived

---

2 Milo C. Frank, *How to Run a Successful Meeting in Half the Time*, (New York: Simon & Schuster, 1989).

consensus with *teamwork*. While it takes a football team to win a game, it is still the individual player who kicks the field goal!

Here is a tip: if you *must* have a safety or loss-prevention committee meeting (because some state governments mandate it), (a) have as few people as possible participate, and (b) try to have this committee meet only once a year!

As to the number of participants in such unavoidable nuisances, being a member of a committee is for many people a matter of great prestige, especially when they are selected from the lower ranks. Therefore, they will do their best to come up with many solutions to prove their mettle. Consequently, keep the number of participants to a minimum.

Another problem is meeting sequence. When a committee is first established, it is easy for members to find obvious shortcomings like, "There is no lighted exit sign over the rear door of warehouse 1," or "The safety guard on the belt sander is broken" However, after the second or third monthly meeting, members are hard pressed to find complaints. Because committees never voluntarily disband, and because it looks silly to have minutes of meetings showing no tangible results, problems begin to be invented, just so that solutions can be found! One begins to hear suggestions like, "Let's relocate door No. 2 in Building C so that in case of a fire, we can shorten the escape route." After all, the human mind—and, if your committee has ten members, as many as ten human minds—can be very resourceful when it comes to proving the need for a committee's existence.

Now management finds itself between a rock and a hard place. Giving in to many superfluous and costly solutions will drain the maintenance staff's labor and cost a lot of money. To refuse to act on the committee's suggestions, however, will expose the company to the possibility of a future lawsuit in case, God forbid, some accident happens and the plaintiff's lawyer can prove that management willfully ignored the recommendations of the safety committee. You can almost see the angry reaction of any jury to such callous behavior!

The other detriment of ignoring committee recommendations is the adverse effect on employee morale. Therefore, planning meetings of this kind only once a year reduces the number of problems faced by management by a factor of twelve, and yet everybody stays happy!

Of course, in the good old days before the intervention of the all-knowing and all-caring government, you had an inspector from your insurance company come around maybe once a year. He was a trained professional, and he would spot shortcomings, write a report, and management would fix the problem(s), if required. Alas, we don't live in such simple times anymore, and we have to do our best to live with the facts of modern life.

Hey, here's a great idea! How about a committee to study and limit the adverse effects of other committees on the fiscal well-being of your company?

CHAPTER

7

Rules for Successful Management

A problem now arises, after you have followed through on my suggestion to reduce the number of managers in your company to a reasonable level. Namely, how do you teach the remaining managers to be more productive and to make sound decisions?

Here are some pointers applicable to owners of businesses, as well as to department heads:

1. Manage your business to make profit your first priority, and then manufacture or sell wid-gets.

2. Try to have only four layers of management in each plant or division.

3. Become—and stay—the master of your computer systems.

4. Design your computer software program (your operating system) to give priority to entering, producing, and shipping customer orders, and *not* to satisfying the accounting department.

5. Don't do or buy things because they are attractive or fashionable. Purchase only what is absolutely necessary! This is especially true for your computer/information system, where the *fad du jour* can be extremely expensive.

6. Solve problems immediately. They will cost you twice as much after one week and four times as much after one month—by which time you've probably lost a customer.

7. Do not manage by committee. Most successful managers are benevolent dictators.

8. Keep your lines of communication short, and avoid meetings like the plague.

9. The most efficient company is a small company (see the chapter on the Law of the Sphere). If you have to grow, then subdivide.

10. Do not ask your subordinates to do things that you would not be able or willing to do your-self.*

11. A well-run department can do all of its required work within an eight-hour day!

12. Do not create departments whose work can be done elsewhere, and assign managers to non-profit-contributing departments on a temporary basis only.

13. Don't fall for fads such as ISO 9001. They can be very expensive. (However, encourage your competitors to do so!) This is not to say that you shouldn't have written records for all *major* tasks, such as order-entry procedure, for example. This might help you to design workable enterprise computer software.

14. If you have any questions, try to solve them using your common sense before going to outside consultants.

15. Train your managers so they are able to run their departments without any external guidance, including your own.

16. Have a *real person* greet your customers when they call your company, and outlaw all voice mail (except, perhaps, for intra-office use).

17. Follow up on a given assignment after about one week's time, as this will ensure that the task is not forgotten by an employee who may not like to do it. A follow-up will convince him that you mean business. The absence of a follow-up will tell him or her that you have forgotten about the assignment—a clear sign that you can be ignored in the future, too.

* While most of the above rules should be self-explanatory, I feel the need to elaborate why you, the boss, should be able to do the work performed by your subordinates. First, it builds morale when employees know that you are more than a remote person in the office or on the shop floor. Second, if there is a problem—with a lack of parts, for example, or machining tolerances—the worker knows that you can understand the problem at hand, and therefore are able to speedily resolve it. Third, by observing the workflow, you can see areas needing improvements. Your underlings will be more comfortable in asking questions regarding their work. Finally, by casually glancing over their shoulders, you can spot errors or mishandling that the person might not even be aware of. This gives you the chance to gently rectify these errors through teaching.

CHAPTER

8

The Coming Demise of the U.S. Automobile Companies

We all dislike the Japanese competition, but we love their cars.

Automobile companies are not exempt from scaling laws, nor should they be. After all, excess size is detrimental to the financial health of such companies, and ultimately will cost consumers. Here is a quandary: a certain minimum company size is necessary in order to secure financing, afford large enough plants and tooling, and create enough sales to establish a viable distribution network; yet, as we shall see, unrestricted growth invites empire building and bloated administration.

What can a company do to increase market share and production without getting bogged down? In my opinion, this can only be done by growing horizontally—that is, by splitting one's company up into a number of truly financially and administratively independent divisions or profit centers.

This was done very effectively at General Motors under the leadership of Alfred Sloan from 1923 to 1946 (note the longevity, unheard of in today's boardrooms). Under his tutelage, competition between each of his divisions—Oldsmobile versus Buick, for example—was at times fiercer than that between GM and its rivals, such as the Ford Motor Company. Remember that if one has, as in this case, twelve independent divisions, one commands, in effect, twelve separate companies. Now, if one of the company presidents performs badly, all you have to do is fire one out of twelve. This is in contrast to a vertically organized firm, where the whole company is in the red if the president messes up.

Alas, Sloan's successors started to follow fashionable trends like pooling resources, combining purchases, centralizing administration, and so on. This in effect robbed their divisions of their independence, all in the name of utilizing "economy of scale." The result was a huge increase in the number administrative layers. It is my understanding that, at the end of 2002, General Motors had about 249,000 employees in the United States, out of which there were only 72,000 factory workers—a mere 29 percent![1] When Roger B. Smith, in the 1980s, tried to reverse the trend, it was already too late. His effort to build a new independent division called Saturn ultimately failed due to the strong opposition of the entrenched GM bureaucracy.[2] After this last attempt to return to basics, the slow demise of this once-proud and largest corporation in the USA began, and the dismantling of its corporate structure began. It continues to this day.

The following is a tabulation of the twelve major world players in the automobile industry for which public data was available.

---

1 2002 General Motors Corp. Annual Report.
2 www.wikipedia.com/The History of General Motors.

COMPANY NAME	NUMBER OF EMPLOYEES	NUMBER OF VEHICLES	$ REVENUE	% PROFIT
General Motors	280,000	8,865,000	198.9 billion	-1.2
Toyota	299,394	7,850,000	179 billion	8.6
Ford Motor	283,000	6,187,000	162.3 billion	-7
Volkswagen	345,000	5,649,000	65.3 billion*	1.5
Nissan	159,771	3,086,000	75.6 billion	NA
Chrysler	83,130	2.545,000	59.4 billion	-2.5
Renault	124,277	2,492,000	55.4 billion*	7.47
Fiat	44,691	1,980,000	30.9 billion*	1.2
Mercedes	382,724	1,653,000	196 billion*	2.1
BMW	106,179	1,370,000	64 billion*	5.4
Porsche	11,910	36,985	9.5 billion*	28.8

* Converted from euros at 1.3 $US per euro

Table 8 -1
Statistical data for selected automobile companies in 2006

The above data are somewhat approximate due to various distorting factors. For example, GM's loss would have been substantially higher had it not been for the profit infusion from its still partly owned General Motors Financing division. Some companies include trucks and buses in their total vehicle count. BMW, for example, also makes motorcycles.

Nevertheless, there is sufficient data to permit us to spot important trends between size and profit, as shown in more detail in the following graphs. Notice that the maker of the smallest number of cars has the highest profit level. On the other hand, Toyota bucks the trend, even as it sits on the verge of being the largest carmaker in the world. Why is it so different from the other "biggies"? Unfortunately, I am not privy to its management structure. However, I suspect that it ensures that each of its five divisions operates profitably. One might argue that Toyota has a roughly 20 percent wage advantage over its U.S. competitors at its U.S.-based assembly plants. This is true, but it's certainly not the whole story. First, its U.S. production accounts for only a small portion of its worldwide sales. Second, assembly accounts for only about 18 percent of the total cost of a car. No ... Toyota must employ a managerial culture that has not yet been under-stood by U.S. companies despite trips by GM's managers to Japan in the 1980s in order to learn its methods. While they were not successful, I assume that they were well-entertained by the geishas.

The trend of decreasing efficiency (or profit) with size becomes very apparent in the following graphs. Figure 8-1 depicts the relationship between yearly revenues and percentage of net operating profit. The trend line clearly shows that, on average, any company with sales above $150 billion tends to be in the red. Toyota and Mercedes-Benz (Daimler) are the only companies to buck the trend.

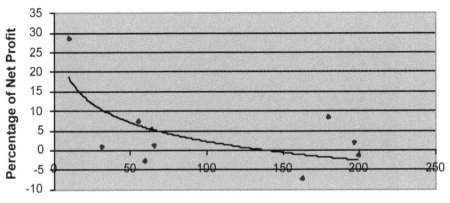

RELATIONSHIP of YEARLY REVENUE and % of NET PROFIT (2006) of AUTOMOBILE COMPANIES

Figure 8-1

A similar trend becomes apparent when one plots the relationship between a company's number of employees and its percentage of profit. This is illustrated in figure 8-2. What is of interest in both graphs is that neither shows an initial up-trend in profit at the low ends—in other words, they do not show the effects of the "economy of scale." It seems as though this might appear only if yearly production were to drop below 30,000 cars per year.

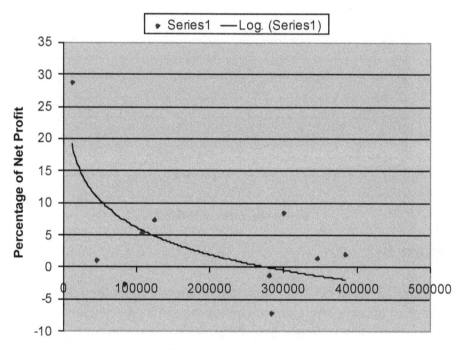

Figure 8-2

There is, of course, an attempt to control costs. However, this is done almost exclusively on the assembly line. There seems to be a fascination with the amount of time it takes to assemble a car. This measurement is then compared with similar time-studies made by competitors. All of these studies are conducted by a special department headed by an assistant vice president, twenty-five managers, and 285 full- and part-time engineers, bookkeepers, and clerks. The results of this $32-million-a-year study are then dutifully published to show de-lighted shareholders that their own company's car-assembly time was within three and a half minutes of that of its nearest competitor.[3] All for a savings of about three dollars per car!

Let's see ... with, say, five million cars per year, this would represent a yearly savings of $15 million. Everybody feels proud about it, without taking the time to consider that it took an overhead expense of $32 million to get it all accomplished. After all, you cannot measure overhead. Direct labor, on the other hand, can be timed to the split second, and therefore can be controlled. Once a bureaucracy gets entrenched, then all attempts to reduce it (the number of salaried employees) fail, because everybody affected pretends to be very busy. Unfortunately, the appearance of personal computers has made this situation worse, because all you have to do is look at your computer monitor to appear busy. There are even books published that instruct redundant employees how to look busy. Here's a tip for good management: Lay off 10 percent of all administrative personnel and see what happens (and make sure that no part-time employees are hired to replace them). The result will surprise you—*nothing* will happen!

---

3 This was a fictitious example, but would you deny that it could very easily be true?

CHAPTER

9

US Airlines—A Model for Self-Destruction

This is the only business where all competitors cut prices the moment they lose money.

The economic health of U.S. airlines started to deteriorate after the government imposed deregulation in the 1970s which theretofore guaranteed a steady and predictable income stream. Financial hemorrhaging started soon thereafter due to competitive pressure and the resultant—almost insane—fare reductions, which in some cases did not even cover the cost of jet fuel.

This cutthroat behavior resulted in the complete demise of a number of world-renowned airlines, such as TWA and Pan Am. Other major airlines—Delta, Continental, and United among them—declared bankruptcy, some even more than once.

While one could blame this on the skyrocketing cost of jet fuel, the cost of financing for new planes, union problems, the 9/11 shutdown, and so on, I feel that management is at least partly to blame for this debacle. It was, and still is, management's inability to manage efficiently when airlines become too large that causes their downfall. As pointed out before, it becomes too difficult to effectively oversee large companies with their ever-increasing reporting layers and associated overhead. Large airlines sometimes realized this problem and tried to split themselves up in order to mimic small, low-cost carriers. Delta is a good example. It sought to increase profit by repainting and rebranding some of its planes under the "Song" banner, while still using the same number of people and facilities. Needless to say, this did not do the trick. Here we had a case of marketing being confused with economics.

Table 9-1 shows several airlines' revenue, net operating income, number of planes in use, and total number of employees at the end of 2006, in some cases following major restructuring.

NAME	REVENUE $ IN BILLIONS	PROFIT %	NO. PLANES	EMPLOYEES
American Airlines	22.58	1.02	670	86,600
United Airlines	18.94	0.13	-	55,000
Delta Air Line	17.17	-36	440	52,260
Continental Air	13.13	2.81	638	41,800
Northwest Air	12.57	-22.65	362	30,080
US Airways	11.56	2.62	800	37,675
Southwest Air	9.09	5.49	481	33,195
Alaska Air Line	3.33	-1.85	114	14,485
Jet Blue Air Line	2.38	-0.04	121	9,250
Air Tran	1.98	1.35	60	7,400
Mesa Air Line	1.34	2.54	199	5,200
Frontier Air Line	1.17	-1.74	67	4,334

| North American Air | 0.83 | -0.8 | 10 | 600 |
| Air Midwest | 0.66 | 0.81 | 20 | 3,076 |

Table 9-1
U.S. Airline Data

I have plotted the data from the above table onto the following graph. The trend is unmistakable. Even accounting for different route structures (more profitable overseas routes versus low-margin domestic routes), for airlines having or not having hubs, and so on, the salary is the same for a gate person, whether the plane loads thirty or 300 people. This is a cost disadvantage for airlines using smaller planes. Midsize airlines (those with around $10 billion in revenues) tend to benefit from the "economy of scale," but thereafter, the profit deteriorates rapidly.

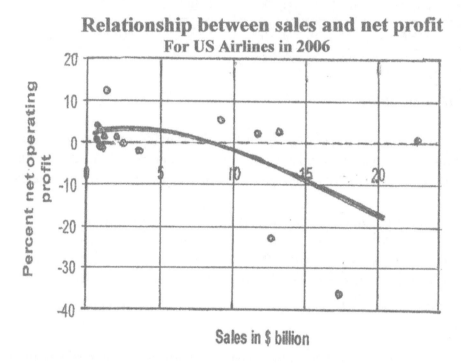

Figure 9-1

The averaging curve in the above graph demonstrates the typical Law of the Sphere shape above the $5 billion sales level, but profit thereafter decreases drastically with growth in sales.

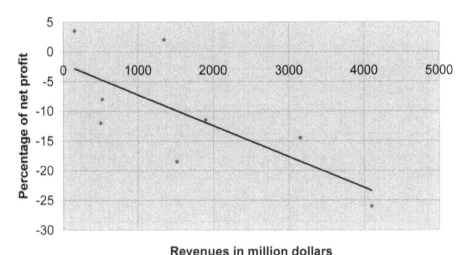

Figure 9-2

Figure 9-2 shows a similar survey from 2003. If anything, it shows an even stronger trend towards losses with increasing revenues.

What causes the deterioration in profitability?

The reason, as always, is due to bloated personnel numbers, usually in administration levels. This assumption is confirmed by the data displayed in figure 9-3, which shows the number of employees per plane plotted against the corresponding percentage of net profit.

NET OPERATING PROFIT v.s. NUMBER OF EMPLOYEES PER PLANE in 2006

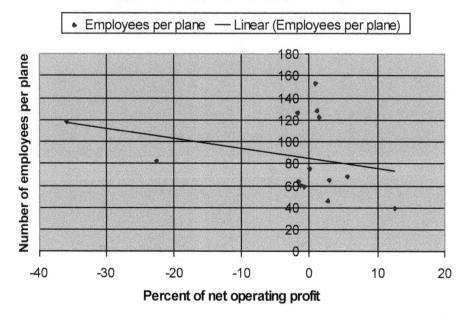

Figure 9-3

Here we see the number of total employees divided by the number of planes owned by a given airline, plotted against the percentage of net operating profit. It is amazing to see how much variation there is. There are some major airlines that need up to 160 people to operate and administer a single plane, whereas others get by very well with only forty people per plane. In all fairness, one must realize that the *very* low numbers may conceal subcontracted baggage-handlers, for example. Nevertheless, we do see an important trend here—that higher profits can only be achieved by pruning personnel expenses. Eighty employees per plane seems to be an optimum number. Note, however, that every airline with less than sixty people per plane shows a decent profit!

We might wonder exactly where all these employees are. I myself have never heard anybody complain about too many flight attendants in an airplane; and, judging by the long lines in front of the airport check-in counters, there is certainly no surplus of counter clerks. To find the answer, we must look inside the offices of the major airlines, where we are likely to find an excess of staffers and managers.

While one must recognize that some of the larger carriers have overseas routes that may demand higher staff requirements, this is compensated for by the higher fare structures on those routes as compared to low domestic fares, and therefore by the resultant higher profit margins of larger international carriers.

What can be done to rectify this picture? First of all, airlines should decrease their level of employment, starting with administration. If possible, they must try to split large firms into several smaller, financially independent airlines. Finally, they must impose a sensible (and generally higher) fare structure that reflects the true cost of operation. If the result is fewer passengers, so be it. The sky is too crowded these days, in any case.

I long for the good old days when everybody sat in a comfortable seat and got to eat decent food served by friendly flight attendants. Today, we have to take off our shoes, get our nail clippers confiscated, and be patted down like common criminals before being herded into a cattle-car that will probably depart late, if at all.

Wouldn't getting rid of the present system be worth a few extra bucks?

CHAPTER

10

Drugs—The More We Spend, the Less We Discover

The nice thing about drugs is that we can always find a second one to counteract the side effects of the first.

Why do pharmaceutical companies discover less even as they spend more? This is a good question. After all, they have invented all kinds of new research tools and techniques, and have even mastered gene splicing. Yet, as we can see from figure 10-2, R&D expenses for manpower and equipment increase, while the number of marketable drugs simultaneously keeps declining exponentially. Even a good company like Abbott Laboratories exhibits this trend. While its R&D expenses increase, its earnings fall, as shown in figure 10-1.

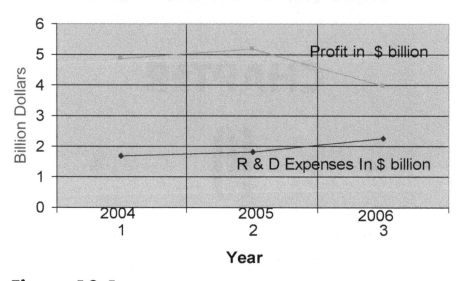

Figure 10-1

Source: *Yahoo Financials*, Abbott Annual Report 2006

In desperation, drug companies try their utmost to extend the lifetime of their patents on old drugs in order to stay profitable.

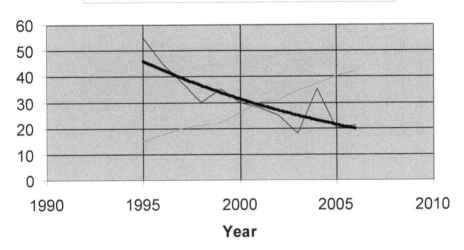

US DRUG COMPANIES R & D EXPENSES vs. NEW DRUGS

— Number of new drugs approved
—— R & D expenses in billions of dollars
— Expon. (Number of new drugs approved)

Figure 10-2
Source: *The Economist*, June 30, 2007, p. 73.

The number of approved new drugs has dropped by 62 percent, from fifty-five to twenty-one, over the last ten years, yet R&D expenses have nearly tripled, from $15 billion to $41 billion, during the same period. Here is a more specific example to illustrate the problem. In the period from December 2004 to December 2006, Bristol-Myers Squibb Co. increased its research expenditure from $2.5 billion to $3.07 billion—a 20 percent increase. Its net profit, however, decreased during that same period from $2.38 billion to $1.59 billion—a 33 percent decrease, as illustrated in figure 10-3.

Bristol-Myer Squibb Co. R & D v.s. Profit

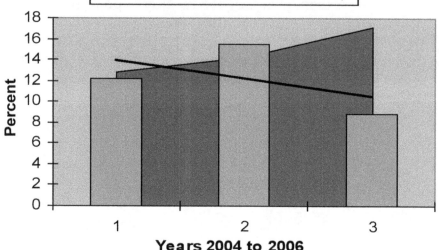

Figure 10-3
Source: Yahoo Financials

If we look back once more to the good old days—say fifty or even a hundred years ago—we see gifted chemists experimenting in laboratories, using intuition, and sometimes stumbling upon good luck to find a cure for some awful disease. Some of them even went so far as to try out new drugs on themselves in order to find out whether they were safe for humans or not.

This all has changed. We now have computer programs that attempt to match various compounds or elements with one another in order to produce something useful. Quite often, the aim of a research project is to manipulate the ingredients of a successful competitor's drug in order to circumvent the competitor's patents. Another way to pretend to bring out something "new" is to simply combine two old drugs and then market the cocktail under a new name.

All this emphasis on technology leads to the need to expend substantial capital for high-tech equipment and the corresponding increase in the skilled manpower to operate it. In other words, the computer operator has replaced the human genius. The result is a widening gap be-tween the cost of capital equipment plus manpower, and the number of newly discovered drugs.

Worse yet is the negative effect of the large number of drug-company mergers during the last decade. Instead of the intended result—that is, a combination of two companies' talent and facilities for better effect— the opposite seems to have occurred. A much larger bureaucracy has stifled nearly all progress and created great inefficiencies, similar to what we have seen in other industries.

A prime example of the deteriorating efficiency (and profitability) in the drug industry is Amgen Inc.

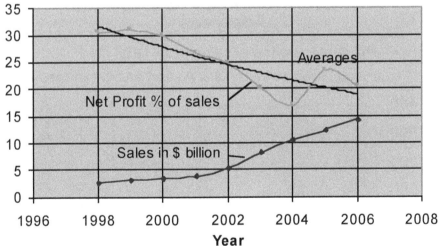

Figure 10-4
Source: *Hoovers Market watch*, Amgen annual report 2004, 2005.

This company, certainly a flagship of the drug industry, has grown substantially over the last twelve years, from $2.7 billion in sales in 1998 to $14.8 billion in 2006, and yet, its net profit as a percentage of sales has decreased from 30.7 to 20.6 percent—a loss of 33 percent in operating efficiency. The company actually posted a *loss* of 28.2 percent in 2002 (while omitted from figure 10-4 for clarity, averages were used for plotting purposes). Let's call this reduction in profit the penalty for growing!

Why did the profit percentage start to decline after 1999? The reason is well explained by the graph in figure 10-5. Here we see that Amgen's sales and administrative expenses increased twice as much as did its sales, thereby eating away at the profit.

Would it not, then, you may wonder, be better for the company to have three divisions, each with $5 billion in sales and each posting a 25 percent profit, than to continue with the cur-rent combined company with its $14.8 billion in sales, but only 20.6 percent in profit? If the company's owners had split it into three parts, they would have carried an additional $650 million to the bank.

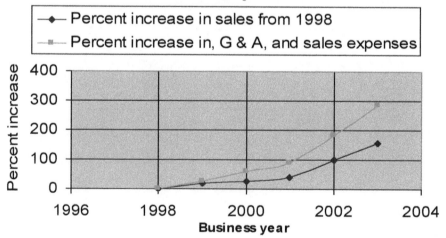

AMGEN, INC. Sales to Overhead Analyses

Figure 10-5

Again, might we not see here the invisible Law of the Sphere at work, which dictates a more rapid rise in the number of non-profit-contributing employees? Consulting our equation from chapter 1, we can calculate the expected percentage of profit as Amgen's sales increase from $2.7 billion in 1998 to $14.3 billion in 2006, using a starting profit of 30.7 percent from 1998 (and an exponential factor of 0.75):

$$\% \text{ profit for } 2006 = (14.3/2.7)^{0.75} \times 30.7 \times (2.7/14.3)$$
$$\% \text{ profit} = 3.49 \times 5.79 = 20.23 \text{ percent.}$$

Guess what Amgen's actual profit was for 2006? It was 20.6 percent (see figure 10-4)! Was this just a lucky guess on my part? On the other hand, if we used an exponential factor of 1 (a linear relationship with constant overhead), the profit would have been 30.7 percent—the same as the company posted in 1998.

Here are other examples: GlaxoSmithKline PLC, the well-known British drug company, in 2006 had a net profit margin of 19.2 percent, with sales of $443,000 per employee. In contrast, the U.S.-based Schering-Plough Corp. only had a profit margin of 10.6 percent. Why? Because its sales per employee only reached $331,343, indicating that it had too many employees. A similar picture is presented by Teva Pharmaceutical Industries. This company had a 20.3 percent net income (not counting special items) on sales of $398,000 per person. This compares with the earnings of Barr Pharmaceuticals, which posted a loss of 25 percent. Then again, Barr's sales per employee only reached $ 281,000. There are, as always, exceptions to the rule. For example, a strong patent position on a popular drug will allow a company to overcharge its customers and thereby hide its inefficiency. Nevertheless, the above examples amplify the fact that excess numbers of employees always eat away at profit.

CHAPTER

11

The Service Industry

Service industries include, among others, banks and insurance companies. All of these require thousands of office workers, yet, aside from buildings and information technology, need few capital investments.

An example is provided by the insurance industry. Its overhead structure is difficult to analyze, because we have no sales volume in the common sense and because its main income is derived not from the insurance business itself, but from return on investments. Nevertheless, we can still see the economy of scale at work in figure 11-1. Small companies certainly have to struggle to make a profit on their pure insurance activities, and it typically takes premium income above $5 billion (in 1998 dollars) in order to break even.

US INSURANCE COMPANIES 1998

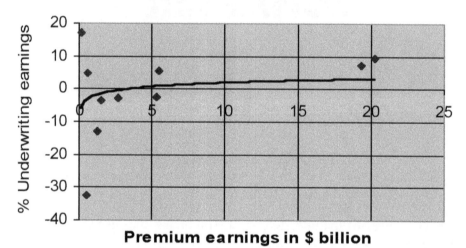

Figure 11-1

Source: *The Value Line Investment Survey*

Yet even here, we find some companies that are not immune to deteriorating efficiencies. An example is the Chubb Corporation, where the percentage of return on money invested decreased by 19 percent—from 7 to 5.7 percent—when its premium income increased by 86 percent from $2.8 billion to $5.2 billion during a ten-year period starting in 1989, as shown in figure 11-2.

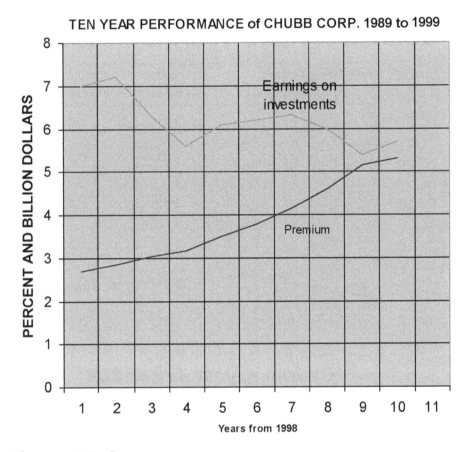

Figure 11-2

Source: *Value Line Investment Survey*

Another example is Columbia Health Care, which had a rapid sales increase starting in 1993 at a rate of 41 percent per year until sales flattened out in 1996. While its profit in dollars increased impressively, its percentage of profit on sales declined from 6.3 to 3.1 percent during this period. This is an indication that the company's overhead outgrew its sales, and that its operating efficiency declined accordingly.

The performance data for this otherwise successful company are plotted in figure 11-3.

TEN YEAR RESULTS of
COLUMBIA HEALTH CARE, 1989-1998

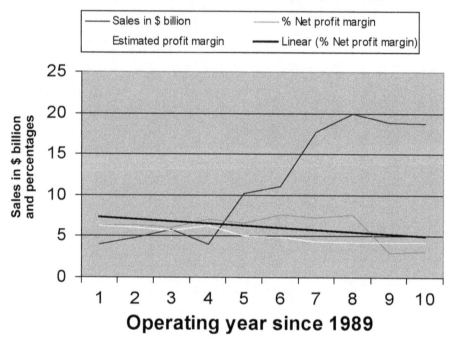

Figure 11-3

Let's consult our Law of the Sphere equation to estimate what the percentage of profit would be in 1998 given the above sales data.

% profit in 1998 = (sales 1998 /sales 1989)^{¾} × % profit 1989
× (sales 1989/ sales 1998)

% profit 1998 = (18.68 / 4.086)^{¾} × 6.3 × (4.086 / 18.68)

% profit 1998 = 4.3 percent

This is very close to the actual rate of profit for 1998 (see graph).

An interesting example of how a company's breakup can work successfully is demonstrated by the results of the American Express Co. As shown in figure 11-4, this company had nearly flat yearly sales between 1989 and 1992 of around $25 billion , with a gradually declining profit margin.

TEN YEAR RESULTS OF AMERICAN EXPRESS CO.

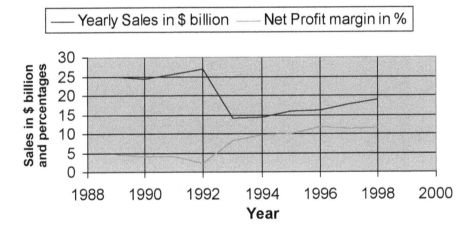

Figure 11-4

Then, between August 1989 and May 1995, the company spun off AMEX Life, Fire-man's Fund Corp., and Lehman Brothers. This led sales to drop by 47 percent, yet profits immediately more than doubled, easily making up for the loss in revenue! In other words, by divesting itself of these divisions, the company increased its profits from $653 million in 1992 to $ 1,380 million in 1994. While the profit margin flattened out after 1996, the company still had a healthy profit of 11.6 percent due to a high sales ratio per employee of $224,000—an indication of good management. This is a prime example of a "good" de-merger.

FINANCIAL RESULTS OF YAHOO! Inc.
for the years 2004 to 2006

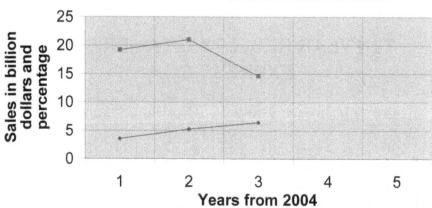

Looking at internet companies, we have Yahoo! Inc., as an example. During the last three years, its revenues grew an impressive 78 percent, yet its operating income decreased from 19.2 to 14.6 percent of total revenue as illustrated by figure 11-5. This is somewhat better than what the Law of the Sphere would have predicted:

$$\% \text{ income } (2006) = (1.78 / 1)^{3⁄4} \times 19.2 \times (1/1.78) = 12.32\%$$

The banking sector also had great financial results between 2004 and 2006 due to the underwriting of merger activities and IPOs of private equity firms, among other sources of in-come. JPMorgan Chase & Co. is a prime example. Its revenues rose an astounding 75 percent, from $56.9 billion in 2004 to $99.8 billion in 2006. Yet its cost of revenue rate (overhead) doubled from 8.1 percent of revenue to 17.0 percent. Despite this increase in overhead, the bank still managed to increase its net income from 7.8 to 13.7 percent. Still, its rate of profit increase at 75.6 percent was less than the rate of increase in overhead at 110 per-cent (see figure 11-6). If the company had somehow managed to keep its costs in proportion to its increase in revenue—that is, at the same 8.1 percent (of revenues) rate of overhead—its net profit for 2006 would have increased by $8.88 billion. This, in turn, would have increased its net profit margin from 13.7 to 22.6 percent! Alas, not being able to do this was perhaps a penalty for growth, as well.

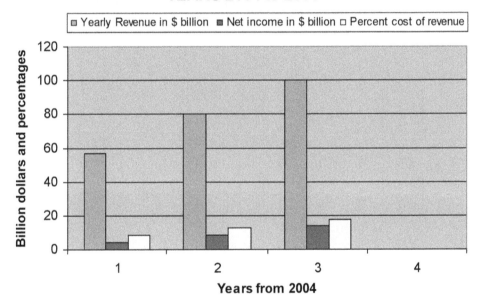

JPMORGAN FINANCIAL RESULTS FOR THE YEARS 2004 to 2006

□ Yearly Revenue in $ billion ■ Net income in $ billion □ Percent cost of revenue

Figure 11-6

Finally, we should not ignore the public utility companies, which, prior to deregulation, enjoyed near-monopolies, with the unrestricted wage and salary expenses these allowed. Alas, that has all changed. The Laclede Group, a nonregulated gas distribution company, supplies us with an example. In the ten years between 1997 and 2007, its revenues

---

1 2007 % profit = $(2.021 / 0.615)^{0.75} \times 5.25 \ (0.615 / 2.021) = 3.9$ %.

nearly quadrupled, from $615 million to $2,021 million. Net income also grew to please the shareholders, from a mere $32 million in 1997 to $49.7 million in 2007.

Yet its operating efficiency, expressed as margins on sales, decreased dramatically, from 5.25 percent of sales to 2.45 percent. This is even less what the Law of the Sphere would have predicted (it assumed 3.9 percent profit[1] in 2007). Laclede's results are shown in figure 11-7. The company apparently added so much new office staff that it had to construct a new steel-and-glass skyscraper to house them all, as is proudly stated in its 2007 annual report.

LACLEDE GROUP Financial Results

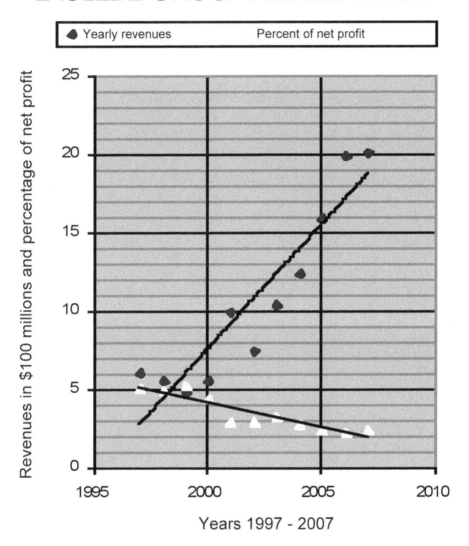

Figure 11-7

CHAPTER

12

The Government Sets an Example

If governments had to operate profitably, they would have expired long ago. Remember, too, that government-legislated assistance is the only help a businessperson is forced to accept.

Government organizations, while having certain budget restraints, are otherwise immune from the need to generate the profits that are all that keep private industries from demise. On the contrary, government budgets are never sufficient, and, as a rule, there is always a cry to increase the budget for the coming year. There always seems to be a dire need for more teachers, firefighters, and so on. Most politicians are ill-qualified to distinguish genuine need from empire building on the part of department heads. Besides, more firefighters mean more voters. If there are insufficient funds for a budget increase, then there is always a tax increase.

Such efforts to increase budgets are observable starting at the smallest village and ending at the federal bureaucracy. In addition, there is always the professed need to help businesses.

Fortunately for our economy, there are only a few businesslike ventures whose efficiency, or lack thereof, could affect us. Examples are the U.S. Post Office and the navy's ship-yards (see chapter 13). This is in contrast to the old Soviet Union, where all industries were owned and operated by the government. We all know the outcome of *that* experiment. It's bad enough if there are unproductive employees in any administration, but inefficiency can be deadly in industries on which we all must depend.

When we examine the federal government, we find that too many reporting layers (see chapter 4) not only create unnecessary manpower, but, what's worse, make their own departments practically defunct.

A case in point is the Central Intelligence Agency. When its operational deficiencies were exposed after the 9-11-2001 attacks, the answer was not to streamline its bureaucracy, but rather to double its manpower! To add insult to injury, the CIA was subsumed into a new super-intelligence organization called the "Office of National Intelligence," which added another layer of almost two thousand bureaucrats. The same thing happened to the FBI, which, with 27,000 employees, already had nine reporting layers before 9/11. Politicians, as do some managers, unfortunately still believe that every problem can be solved by adding more employees. In fact, this will seldom do the trick. This reminds me of Frederick P. Brooks's saying, "Adding man-power to a late [software] project makes it later." He also said, "The bearing of a child takes nine months, no matter how many women are assigned."

Another sad example was the bungling by the Homeland Security Department of the response to Hurricane Katrina in 2005. That catastrophe would likely not have been as bad as it was had the president simply left FEMA alone instead of bundling it and other departments into a super-bureaucracy with layer upon layer of often-unqualified chiefs and an unfathomable chain of command. Such incomprehensible merger mania not only infects the federal bureaucracy, but that of local governments as well. School boards are a prime example. Sometimes, the school boards of two separate towns decide to combine—ostensibly to save money. However, what usually happens next is that a brand new and larger school building has to be erected. Next, the kids from either of the old schools have to be bused to the newer, more distant, location. And what about the advertised cost savings? The giveaway is that not a single teacher or administrator will be laid off after the school merger. On the contrary, because a new school building has been planned for the future—a building that has to have more rooms than those of the two old schools combined—there is now ample space for additional administrative personnel, who will all be hired in due course. The increased cost will be covered by the next school budget.

CHAPTER
13

Running an Enterprise, Government Style

Taxes expand to cover a government's losses.

We tend to belittle inefficient government agencies or enterprises when they are run so badly, because their failures have been reported so often that we have grown numb to them. It is true that any inefficiency will always be covered up by tax money, contrary to private enterprise, where bankruptcy is the inevitable end of such folly (unless a business has a monopoly, in which case a price increase will serve to cover up bad management decisions). It is our own fault as citizens that we allow governments to operate inefficiently. The unfortunate fact, however, is that we can do little about it. Government agencies will drown your complaints in endless hearings until you give up. The cover-up starts with the local chamber of commerce that avoids rocking the boat, knowing full well that the closure of a government facility would be bad for local businesses. It extends to unions that are afraid to lose members, and therefore income. The next bunch to cling to the status quo are the congressmen, senators, and governors, who are all afraid to lose votes if workers are laid off or the local economy gets hurt.

Inefficient government businesses are sometimes kept running without any real purpose at all. (The same can be said of some departments of larger private companies.) A case in point: My factory was located not too far from a navy shipyard that overhauled one, or sometimes two, nuclear submarines at a time. This yard used to employ 8,200 full-time plus 800 part-time workers. The part-timers constituted a ploy by the yard's management to pull the wool over Congress's eyes. These 800 employees would be hired two months before the budget review process. Then, four months later, they would be laid off *as a sign of good will toward Congress* ("See how efficient we are? We promise to do the same job even after eliminating 10 percent of the workforce!" Applause follows.) The local papers even advertised in their want ads that the positions to be filled were only part time jobs that would last only six months. Nonetheless, this ruse worked for many years!

When guests visited my company, I would sometimes take them to a restaurant on the river across from the navy yard. After pointing out the facilities and explaining their functions, I would give my guests a test, of sorts. I would ask them to guess how many workers they thought it would take to repair two nuclear submarines, taking into consideration that hardly more than fifty people could *work* in such tight surroundings without bumping into one another. I would also caution them to consider that the yard was not a moneymaking enterprise, but a government-run facility. The answers from these mostly very experienced people (some of whom were company presidents themselves) ranged from 300 to a maximum of 1,200 employees. They were stunned when I told them that the true number was 8,200!

With the end of the Cold War and the decommissioning of many submarines, the yard has finally had to make some cutbacks, and its current employment stands at around 3,800 (for a while, there wasn't a single submarine in the yard). So, assuming that all these people aren't being paid merely for political or social reasons, what do they all do? The answer may surprise you. They are all very busy!

Here is a breakdown of the yard's various major departments and its labor, as of 1996:

Department	Number of Employees
Engineers (quality and process)	296
Administration and Accounting	578
Entertainment	27
Electronic Data System	358
Training and Education	225
Public Relations	53
Machine Shop	278
Power Plants	136
Yard Facilities	120
Maintenance	178
Human Resources	203
Security (other than U.S. Marine guard)	58
Navy Liaison	125
Congressional Liaison	37
Procurement	413
Communication	62
Print Shop	112
Warehousing/Storage	155
Yard workforce	395
(people who actually *perform work* inside a submarine)	
TOTAL	**3,809**

As you can see, everybody is not only gainfully employed, but kept very busy, with some overtime thrown in to make up for time lost due to vacation and illnesses. This, of course, does not take into account the occasional goof-off who hides in the supply room to read *Playboy Magazine*.

Oh yes, it may surprised you, but there really is a department for entertainment, with its own 560-seat theater! I suppose that it was needed in case employees get too bored.

Now, I must hasten to say that the above organizational chart is entirely the product of my imagination. I know quite well that this type of data is highly classified. The last thing I need is the FBI knocking on my door.

Work that you and I might consider unproductive could be of very high value to the affected employees. Consider, for example, the three-year (true) study by the yard's engineering department on how to increase the yard's efficiency. The outcome of these many thousands of man-hours was a new procedure whereby a yard worker would look up the drawing for a given piece of equipment and *then* go inside the submarine to take the part out. In the old system, they would go inside the submarine, look at the part, and then go to get the drawing. I kid you not!

Consider the machinist I once hired as a part-time worker. His main job was working the night shift at the navy yard, were he was assigned to a gear-hobbing machine.[1] Like his counterpart during the day shift, he didn't actually perform any work other than to stand by just in case, somewhere in the world, a propulsion gear broke. This gave the worker ample rest for his day job with me. In case of a gear failure, a "code red" would be sent to the yard by e-mail, which would signal the worker to push the Start button on his machine and produce a new gear.

Simply placing a spare gear in the warehouse would do no good. Because gears break only very infrequently, chances are that this spare gear would lie on the shelf for more than a year, and under navy regulations, equipment that is not used within a year is to be discarded. So you see, it sometimes makes perfectly good sense to pay people to do nothing!

It hasn't always been this way. During World War II, the yard was one of the most efficient production facilities for diesel-powered submarines. If we go back farther, we find a very dramatic decrease in the ratio between effective and supportive personnel. For example, according to

---

1 A machine to cut teeth into a gear, in this case used to drive the propeller

a report in the *Army and Navy Chronicle*[2] dated 8/20/1840, the budget of the French Navy was listed as 7,539,700 Francs for officers, 19,066,000 Francs for enlisted men, and only 666,500 Francs for administrative personnel. In other words, only 8.8 percent of the total were administrative personnel expenses![2]

In his famous book *Parkinson's Law*,[3] C.N. Parkinson related that in the British Navy dockyards, the number of supportive personnel grew from 5.7 percent of the total in 1914 to 7.3 percent in 1928—an increase of 28 percent in fourteen years. The trend to increase the number of supportive employees seems to have accelerated in more recent times, perhaps due to the demands of increasing communications (after all, in 1914, there was only Morse code and the telephone, and now we have e-mail). In any case, Parkinson found that the British staff of the Colonial Office, for example, increased by an average of 5.89 percent per year between 1935 and 1954. This increase happened despite the fact that most of Britain's colonies gained independence during this period.

We, of course, have the same problem here in the USA. In a recent editorial in *USA Today*, it was stated that defense department mismanagement increased the percentage of overhead from 33 to 66 percent over a period of fifteen years. At that rate, the overhead percentage will be 83 percent in another fifteen years (around 2015). In other words, only $17 of every $100 appropriated will be used to purchase actual hardware. The rest will go to overhead expenses according to our Law of the Sphere, employed here to predict the future based on the last fifteen years of figures. Any further money allocated by Congress to "fight waste" will do no good, because this money will only add another layer of auditors on top of the pile, leading to an even higher rate of overhead!

What does all this mean to us as businesspersons? Well, if thousands of people can exist in government, toiling to communicate, teach, support, and otherwise keep each other occupied, then the same can happen,

---

2 Army and Navy Chronicle, (Washington, D.C, 1840)
3 Parkinson, C.N., Parkinson's Law, (Boston: Houghton Mifflin Co., 1975)

perhaps on a smaller scale, within certain departments of private companies. One type of private industry that comes close to operating like a government enterprise is the public utility. Prior to deregulation, it made no difference how efficient a utility was or how bloated its staff was. The state utility commissions would always allow you a rate in-crease to cover expenses, so that a 10 percent profit was always guaranteed. Alas, this is no longer true, and deregulation has forced utilities to adapt.

Here is an example: A small utility company in Vermont found itself in the red after de-regulation and foundered on the edge of bankruptcy. It had fourteen senior executives and 400 employees eating away whatever profit there was. After cutting its dividend and weathering threats made by its banks, its management finally came to their senses and made drastic cuts in employment. Now there are only 196 employees and six senior executives, and earnings have increased from -1.3 percent to +5 percent after taxes. Now sales are up to $1.3 million per employee, from only $400,000. This again shows that even in private enterprise, an amazingly large number of employees are really *not needed!*

It's quite remarkable that following massive layoffs in U.S. industry during and after the last recession, in 1992, the profits of most of these cost-cutting companies exploded, which in turn led to one of the biggest bull markets the United States has ever had. Internal vigilance by management and tight control of budgets are necessary to avoid uncontrolled growth in bureaucracy that, like a cancer, can destroy a healthy organism from within.

Don't be fooled by the fact that all employees in a given department are working hard. The only meaningful question is: Does their work produce profit? In the above example of the navy yard, the only effective employees were those 395 people actually doing the repair work (10.4 percent of the total). And yet, the yard would still exist, with its employees still working eight hours a day, if those 395 effective employees were laid off! This is the lesson we can draw from such an organization: the size of an organization or department has nothing to do with its stated purpose. Or, as C.N. Parkinson so eloquently stated, "Work expands to fill the time available."

With government activities tending to expand over the years and the private sector not supplying enough fuel in the form of taxes, as was the case in the early 1990s, the "take" by the government from the Gross Domestic Product (GDP) increases, percentage-wise.

Contrary to the pronouncements of our liberal politicians, extra spending does *not* increase growth in our overall economy.

An article in the *Wall Street Journal* dated April 10, 1989, which was based on a study by a Professor Gwartney of Florida State University, showed data that I have reproduced in figure 12-1. The data from various countries show conclusively that if taxes are too high (if government spends too much of GDP), then the resultant economical expansion is very meager.

As a matter of fact, the five most rapidly expanding economies in 1995 (Hong Kong, Singapore, South Korea, Taiwan, and Thailand) had only 20 percent of GDP taken by their governments. Highly taxed countries such as the United States or the United Kingdom had only a fraction of the rate of growth experienced by the low-taxed countries. It is no accident that the countries with the highest tax rates as a percent of GDP are also much larger in size than those with the smaller tax rates, confirming, once again, that *smaller is better.*

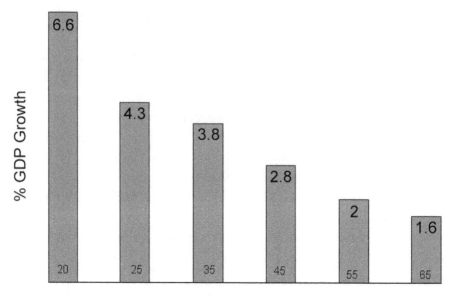

Figure 13-1

Size of government and annual growth of real GDP for OECD countries: 1960 to 1996.

It is obvious from the above graph that if a government takes less money in the form of taxes out of the economy, then that economy will experience a higher growth rate. A good ex-ample is that of Singapore (represented by the bar farthest to the left). Here, the total tax rate was 20 percent of GDP. This resulted in an annual growth rate of 6.6 percent of GDP. Currently, China has the highest growth rate, with about 11 percent of GDP. Leaving aside a benign tax rate, one has to wonder how much of the country's business income stays unreported, and there-fore deflates the official tax rate while adding to the real growth of GDP.

CHAPTER

14

Concluding Summary

The data presented herein supports the observation that some companies, like living organisms, experience limits in the growth of their profit margins. While not linked to biological or physical laws, there is nevertheless a scaling effect that limits such growth in a given firm. Such scaling effects, or laws, as suggested in this book indicate the negative effects on percentage of profit by diverting growth rates from production to administrative employees. From the researched data emerges an indication that profit starts to deteriorate, for many firms, when total employment exceeds 5,000 persons and the number of reporting layers exceeds six. However, such rules do not apply for companies that have high capital investments but low levels of employment, such as refineries, power plants, and chemical plants. With these, administrative expenses are typically below 5 percent of yearly turnover. Therefore, any reduction in overhead has only a small impact on profitability. Yet even here, we see lower profit levels with increases in size. Also, the given rules will not fully apply to large retail chains in which each store represents a separate profit center, franchise businesses, and other companies that are highly divisionalized (i.e., horizontally structured). As logic suggests,

and as data confirms, profits will rise if there are fewer employees producing certain goods. In other words, net profit is typically proportional
to the amount of sales per employee. This may in part be due to the use of
more efficient production equipment at the plant level, but quite often it
is due to the reduction of numbers of administrative personnel in a given
firm. Finally, one must distinguish between organic growth of companies
(as manifested through an increase in market share) and increases in sales
volume primarily caused by inflation. Only the former will benefit from
a switch from a vertical to a horizontal mode of growth in order to avoid
the detrimental effects here discussed.

One may ask whether there is a limit to company growth. The answer
is yes, and this will manifest itself when any increase in operating profit
is offset by an even larger increase in administrative expenses.

About The Author

Hans Baumann is a world renowned Engineer specializing in Control Equipment and acoustic. Through his career, and in addition to starting his own manufacturing company, he served as Corporate Vice-President for such firms as Emerson Electric and the former Studebaker-Worthington Corp. both in Europe and in the US. He is a prolific inventor with over 150 US and foreign patents to his credit. INTECH Magazine named him "one of fifty most influential industrial innovators" and his designs garnered numerous awards in the US, France, Germany, and Japan. Besides over 110 articles and scientific papers, Dr. Baumann published a number of technical books, the acclaimed management book "The Ideal Enterprise" and a history book entitled "Hitler's Fate". He lectured at Universities in the US, Japan, and Korea and is an advisor to the Dean of the UNH Business school. In addition, he served as Advisor on Foreign Trade to the Governor of New Hampshire.

After his undergraduate studies in Germany, he attended Western Reserve University under a grant from the US Marshall Plan, received a Ph.D. in Mechanical Engineering and is a member of Sigma Xi, The Scientific Research Society.

Appendix

"What Do They Mean When They Say...?"—An Irreverent Glossary

"A rose by any other name would smell as sweet."
—William Shakespeare

Not too long ago, the government started to define heretofore clearly understood words in new verbiage in order to obscure their true meaning. For example, the formerly to-the-point "War Department" became the more benevolent-sounding "Defense Department." Unfortunately, corporate America has followed suit, sometimes simply by trying to be politically correct.

While most of you will be familiar with at least some of these newly minted expressions, I thought that it might be helpful to have some translations handy. They should help you understand what is truly being said in any meeting you attend, especially when you are con-fronted with unknown acronyms. I thought it might also be helpful to explain, briefly, the functions and purposes of major enterprises.

153

A

Action Item
A work assignment for a committee member. Also serves to help write agenda for next meeting.

Adaptable Employee
One who changes jobs a lot.

Adept at Office Organizations
To be familiar with Microsoft Office

Airline Operations
Involving a reduction in airfares once an airline loses money.

Auto Companies (U.S.)
Once-profitable enterprises going broke while believing that bigger is better.

B

B2C
A business that sells to consumers.

Bankruptcy
When there is no more money left and you are at the mercy of your creditors.

Bad Mergers
Mergers where the bonuses of the merged company's management go up, but the share price of the owners goes down.

Banks
Private enterprises in business to lend your money to people you have never met at a steep fee.

Benchmarking
A look at what your competitors are doing.

Best-cost producer
The best-qualified supplier, not necessarily the cheapest one.

Board of Directors
A committee that supervises the company president, and whose members are elected by the shareholders, but usually are selected by the president. This limits their effectiveness.

Budget
A yearly sales target selected by management, seldom adhered to if not for price increases and inflation.

Business Ethics
See Criminal Law

C

Capital Asset
Something you buy that can be depreciated. Affects only your cash flow, not your profit.

Casual Work Atmosphere
A workplace in which the pay is too low for you to bother dressing up.

Chief Information Officer (CIO)

Top manager for computer systems. This person is supported by a number of consultants for technical know-how.

Co-branding

An advertising campaign that uses the brand name of a second firm (usually one with a more recognizable name than yours).

Committee Organization

Structure in which groups of individuals hold joint authority and responsibility, and in which no single person can be blamed for anything.

Computer Aided Design (CAD)

Using a mouse instead of a pencil.

Competition

A war between companies conducted by other means.

Cost of Quality

A misnomer. Should be: Cost of no quality.

Communication Skills

Ability to read and send e-mail.

Competitive Salary

Remaining competitive by paying lower wages than the competition.

Creative Selling

The art of being a successful salesman while having a high moral tolerance.

Cross-Functional Teamwork

Different departments trying to work together on a common project. A good way to create delays.

Consumer Satisfaction

A temporary reduction in the number of complaints about your products and service.

D

Delegation

The assignment of unpleasant work to others.

Deadline

Something to force the completion of a never-ending project.

Differentiation

Why my product is better than yours.

Disintermediation

Crossing out the mediation clause in your contract. Means that you have a potential lawsuit that makes the attorneys happier.

Drug companies

Firms vying to outspend each other in failing to invent new drugs.

Downsizing

Laying off employees—usually those with higher salaries and more experience.

Duties will vary
You may have several bosses

E

Empowering
Occasionally letting you decide when to go to lunch.

Enhance the Bottom Line
Reduce the cost.

Entrepreneurship
An ability lacking in most managers.

**Enterprise System
(also: Enterprise Computing)**
A digital version of how a company is thought to be organized.

Environmental Technician
Janitor

E-Mail
A method of communicating via computer keyboard instead of speaking directly to the person in the next office.

Executive Assistant
Secretary

F

Fast-Paced Company
One that has no time to train its employees.

Federal Reserve Bank
An independent banking system established to support government policies by distributing newly printed money (see: Cause of Inflation).

G

Government
An administrative system that, contrary to private enterprises, guarantees full employment while ignoring deficits.

Gross Domestic Product (GDP)
A fictitious number published by the government as an excuse to spend more money.

H

Hardware
The portion of a computer system that you can actually touch.

Horizontal Business Organization
A company composed of a number of financially independent subsidiaries.

Human Resources Department
Personnel Department

Human Resources
Employees

I

IT
Information Technology

Income Statement
Your income and expenses.

Informal Communication Channels
Gossip

Insurance Companies
Companies that, for a fee, insure you against all kinds of hazards, except those hidden in the fine print of your policy.

Integrated Marketing Communication (IMC)
Combining all advertising

Internal Customer
An employee from a different department.

Internet
A computerized form of simultaneous communication between single or multiple number of persons (or computers) done by interconnecting different computers in a network, usually via telephone wires (see E-Mail); mostly used for other than business purposes.

Inventory Control
The art of balancing the purchasing of parts against the shipment of finished goods.

IT Manager
See Manager of Information Technology

ISO 9000
A clever method of consultant enrichment.

J

Just-in-Time (JIT)
Near perfect execution of inventory control, where actual in-house inventory approaches zero.

L

Leadership
An assumed management ability.

Legacy System
An older computer program file that a newer program has to be able to read. Example: Windows 98 has to be able to read a file written on Windows 95.

Local Area Network (LAN)
A system that connects a number of computers in a given area.

Loss Prevention Specialist
Security guard

M

Market Research

An effort to collect data from customers and competitors to help launch your product. To be effective, such research should not be conducted by the person promoting the product.

Market Capitalization

The value of all the shares of a company based on hype rather than earnings.

Manager of Information Technology

The person you beg for help when your computer crashes.

Macroeconomics

The study of a company's finances in view of the national economy.

Merger

The joining of two companies for the benefit of the involved management.

M-commerce

Mobile electronic commerce. Buying books via cell-phone or wireless computer.

Microeconomics

The study of whether or not your boss will give you a raise.

Mission Statements

Modern form of company logos. Can be found on the backs of business cards.

Morale

The mental attitude of employees, which can be influenced by communication, raises, or bonuses.

N

Negative Deficit

Profit

Negative Economic Growth

Recession

Not-for-profit Organization

Tax exempt enterprises with unusually high advertising budgets and management salaries.

O

Order Processing

Order entry.

Order Fulfillment

The entire process from order entry to the shipment of goods.

Organization Chart

A listing of company managers and their relationship to each other; often used as an excuse for not helping out in another department.

Outsourcing

Purchasing goods from somebody else.

Ownership
Taking ownership means you have been as-signed a task.

P

Parent Company
An organization that owns a subsidiary.

Performance Appraisal
A method of filling out forms to either deny or grant raises to an employee.

Portfolio Manager
Stockbroker.

Positive Cash Flow
Making money without paying taxes.

Price Adjustment
Price increase.

Procurement
Purchasing.

Problem-Solving Skills
A prerequisite in a disorganized company.

Product Differentiation
Convincing your customers that your products are better than those of your competitors, even though the price might be higher (see Creative Selling).

Product Launch
Introduction of a new product to the market. Usually done before the product is ready.

Product Liability
A means to extract money from firms or insurance companies, usually based on assumed product defects.

Production Planning
Telling the machine shop how many parts to produce, or the purchasing department how much inventory to buy

Pride in Work
Not to be mistaken for "blaming others for my errors."

Productivity
A means to determine profitability; also, an index published by the Labor Department in order to embellish GDP numbers.

Pure Play
A business that sells only via the Internet and does not own a store, or one that sells from a catalog.

R

Re-engineering
Usually refers to the downsizing the company whose profit is low.

Reverse Engineering
A fancy way to copy your competitor's products.

Research and Development
Efforts, usually by a team of engineers, to design a new product from specifications developed by a marketing team. Success usually is inversely proportional to the number of team members.

Resume
Documents written by employees when company morale is low.

S

Sales Associate
Salesclerk

Self-Management Team
A group of employees on their own if their manager is absent.

Seller's Market
A market in which the price of goods can be set without worrying about competitors.

Service Technician
Repairman

Social Responsibility
Management's actions to combat (usually) government-perceived misbehavior.

Synergism
An understanding between presidents of soon-to-be merged companies of how to divide bonuses.

Software
Invisible instructions that tell your computer what to do. Usually written by persons unfamiliar with your business, and typically obsolete at time of purchase.

Solution
A piece of software that is supposed to solve all your problems.

Statistical Quality Control
A fancy name to express the average dimensional error in a machined part's dimensions.

Strategic Alliance
A usually long-term purchasing agreement between a seller and a buyer based on a guaranteed price discount.

Strategic Planning
Usually a five-year sales and financial performance forecast.

Ship on Time
Shipping goods on the day promised.

SWOT Analysis
Assessment of company's strengths and weaknesses, usually through the eyes of a consultant.

T

Task-Specific Role
The execution of action item by a committee member.

Team
A group of people assigned to a project and devoid of any personal responsibility for the task.

Team Cohesiveness
Camaraderie typically enhanced by joint golf games.

Team Leadership
Having the responsibilities of a manager, without the pay.

Telemarketing
People telephoning you during dinner.

Territory Managers
Outside salesmen

Total Quality Management (TQM)
The public expression of management's commitment to the quality of its product. Usually an action of last resort.

V

Variable Cost
Cost of labor and material usually overshadowed by fixed cost (administrative expenses).

Vertical Organization Structure
Companies whose organization structure looks like a Christmas tree, and where overhead grows exponentially with size.

Viral Marketing
When somebody who sells you something talks you into advertising it to your friends and relatives.

Voice Mail
Form of communication whereby you can carry on a conversation without ever speaking directly to the person you called.